D0052811

The
SLEDGE PATROL

The
SLEDGE PATROL

A WWII Epic of Escape, Survival, and Victory

David Howarth

The Lyons Press
Guilford, Connecticut
An imprint of The Globe Pequot Press

To buy books in quantity for corporate use
or incentives, call **(800) 962–0973**
or e-mail **premiums@GlobePequot.com**.

Copyright © 1957 by David Howarth

ALL RIGHTS RESERVED. No part of this book may be reproduced or
transmitted in any form by any means, electronic or mechanical, including
photocopying and recording, or by any information storage and retrieval
system, except as may be expressly permitted in writing from the publisher.
Requests for permission should be addressed to The Globe Pequot Press, Attn:
Rights and Permissions Department, P.O. Box 480, Guilford, CT 06437.

Originally published in 1957 by The Macmillan Company, New York.
First Lyons Press edition, 2001

The Lyons Press is an imprint of The Globe Pequot Press.

Library of Congress Cataloging-in-Publication Data is available on file.

ISBN: 978-1-59921-322-4

Printed in the United States of America

10 9 8 7 6 5 4 3 2 1

CONTENTS

PART ONE

Eskimoness   *vi*

PART TWO

Sabine Island   *31*

PART THREE

The Encounter   *50*

Author's Note   *218*

PART ONE

ESKIMONESS

1

ON THE north-east coast of Greenland, on a point of land called Eskimoness, six hundred miles beyond the Arctic Circle, there used to be
a wooden house. It is burnt down now, and there is nothing left there
except a small outhouse which escaped the fire. The house was built
as a scientific station, but in the early spring of 1943 it became the
centre of a fight: a fight which began near the house and then ranged
for four hundred miles up and down the beautiful desolate coast.

There were seven men living in the house at the time, four Danes,
one Norwegian and two Eskimos, though some of them were away
from home on dog-sledge journeys. They had spent the winter there.
They were cut off from the rest of the world except for the radio, and
their nearest neighbours, so far as they knew, were in another house
on an island called Ella, two hundred miles to the southward. North
of them, there was nobody at all. But they were not oppressed by their
isolation; they were used to it, and they rather liked it. The Eskimos

had been born to it, and the Europeans had all spent other winters in the arctic. Each of them, in his own way, was in love with the arctic, as most men are who know it well enough to face its dangers with confidence and put up with its discomfort. They were all aware of its beauty, and its peace and freedom, and they had all been happy there that winter, enjoying the primitive excitement of hunting dangerous animals, and their own mastery of the technique of living in the extreme cold, and the peculiar exultation of driving dog teams on the sea-ice in the arctic night.

In the arctic all men have a common enemy in the climate, and it has always been an unbroken tradition there that men are friends; and so it seemed incredible to the men at Eskimoness when they found themselves, at the end of that winter, suddenly faced with human enemies, forced to hunt men instead of polar bears and foxes, and to discover what it felt like to be hunted.

This is simply the story of the fight which began there on the afternoon of March 11th, 1943, when one of the seven men, to his amazement, saw a human footprint in the snow, and which only ended when the ice broke up in June. But to explain why the men were at Eskimoness and what they were doing there, one has to go back much earlier than that; in fact, to make the story complete and place it in its setting, one ought to go back very briefly for exactly a thousand years.

2

GREENLAND BELONGS to Denmark. Its history is long, and some of it is pathetic. It was given its strangely unsuitable name by Eric the Red, a Norwegian Viking, who discovered it in the tenth century, and was the father of the man who discovered America. Probably he called it Greenland as a kind of propaganda, because he wanted to persuade other people from his home in Iceland to follow him to found a settlement; but perhaps, after the snow and black lava fields of Iceland, the part of Greenland which he saw did really look green to him. He landed on the south-west coast in summer; and on that stretch of coast, though not on any other, when the snow disappears in spring, a strip of grassland emerges between the barren mountains and the sea.

At all events, he did establish a settlement, eighty years before the Battle of Hastings. Before the settlers landed, South Greenland was uninhabited, but they found the remains of the houses of an unknown race of human beings. These were Eskimos, who had lived there in a previous age, but then had died out or migrated to the north. It was six centuries more before a living Eskimo was seen by a European.

For several hundred years the settlement in Greenland prospered, a peaceful Christian community with its own Bishop and Parliament. But it was never self-supporting. There was no timber for building boats or houses, and the settlers were never able to grow corn. For these necessities they had to depend on ships from Scandinavia.

Towards the middle ages, the wealth and power of the Scandinavian kings declined, and the effort and expense of organizing expeditions to the distant colony became too much for them. By the end of the four-teenth century a ship from the outside world was only seen in Greenland once or twice in a man's lifetime. In 1492, the Pope observed that no ship had been to Greenland for eighty years. The settlement was forgot-ten, except as a historical curiosity; and in the settlement, where three or four generations had passed since a ship had last been sighted, one must suppose that the outside world had been almost forgotten too.

Lately, the graves and houses of the Greenland settement have been excavated. The people's burials show that they clung to their Christian faith; but their skeletons show how their health and strength began to fail. Their Viking ancestors had been tall and strong, but the fifteenth century colonists were tiny, men under five feet and the women under four feet nine. They suffered from tuberculosis and undernourishment, and perhaps from inbreeding, and their expectation of life was less than thirty years.

There is also some evidence that about this time the climate of Greenland began to change. It got colder, the glaciers spread down towards the pastures, and the summers became too short to ripen crops. The coldness brought the arctic animals, polar bears and seals and walrus, farther south; and with them came a new migration of Eskimos, who live by hunting and do not depend on crops. Some time in the sixteenth century, in this unfriendly land, surrounded by primitive pagan people of another race, the very last of the forgotten

Christian settlers died. H may well have believed, as he lay there dying alone, that he was the last Christian in the world.

But the history of Greenland made a fresh start in 1721. A Danish missionary called Hans Egede went there in that year to try to find the lost colony; but by then, it was probably two hundred years too late. There was nobody there except Eskimos. Hans Egede stayed there to preach, and ever since then the Danes have worked hard to bring the benefits of civilisation to the Eskimos and to spare them from its disadvantages. They have had their difficulties, but on the whole the Danish rule in Greenland has been a model of colonial policy. The population is much bigger than it was two hundred years ago. The people are prosperous after their own fashion, devoutly Christian, and perfectly peaceful and contented; and the country is not a colony now, it is a part of Denmark.

But through all these centuries of history, civilisation only touched one side of Greenland, the mere fringe of the west coast. The west coast is free of ice for several months each summer, and it still has its patches of fertile ground. There are several small towns there now, and altogether over twenty thousand people, a mixed race of Eskimo and Danish origin who do not call themselves Eskimo or Danish, but simply Greenlanders.

But the whole of the interior of the country is an enormous ice-cap which does not support life of any kind; and on the east coast, the nearest side to Europe, a sea current from the north brings drifting polar ice right down to the Atlantic, so that ships can only reach that side of Greenland for six weeks or so in the autumn of every year. For this reason, the vast stretches of the eastern coast were not explored till modern times. It is still almost uninhabited, and always will be. This coast is 1600 miles long; its great fjords, which are frozen for ten months of every year, lead 200 miles inland; its mountains are nearly as high as the Alps, and much more extensive. Yet in the whole of this tremendous area, there are only two villages.

Four hundred miles up from its southern end is the settlement of Angmagssalik, which has a population of 1500, of almost pure Eskimo blood. Four hundred and fifty miles beyond Angmagssalik is Scoresby Sound, with a population of about three hundred. Beyond Scoresby Sound is the territory of north-east Greenland, seven hundred more miles of beautiful mountainous coast where nobody lives at all except a few solitary hunters and the radio operators in four weather stations.

To Europeans, the whole of Greenland seems a far-away northern country; in the settled parts of Greenland, they think of Scoresby Sound as a wild and distant outpost; and in Scoresby Sound itself, the north-east coast is as remote as the Hebrides are to a Londoner. Up there, three hundred and fifty miles north of Scoresby Sound, is Eskimoness, only distinguished from tens of thousand of other projecting rocks by having a name, and the ruins of a house on it.

3

WHEN GERMANY invaded Denmark on April 9th, 1940, nobody gave much thought to the colony of Greenland. After a time, Britain sent forces to occupy Iceland and the Faroe Islands, Denmark's other colonies; but America was still neutral in the war, and Greenland was too remote to interest the European powers.

But the invasion of Denmark had a profound effect in Greenland. There were a good many Danes there in the colonial administration, and they were just as astonished and bewildered by the German invasion as the Danes at home in Denmark; in fact, on the whole, they may have been more bewildered, because they only heard contradictory German and American reports of what was happening, and had no chance to see it for themselves. The junior members of the administration were mainly concerned at being cut off so suddenly from their families, and were mainly worried by thoughts of the fate of their friends at home. But the governor of the colony was also faced with a constitutional problem. The King of Denmark had ordered all Danes to submit to the German occupation, because it was obviously impossible to prevent it. In fact, he had been advised to submit by the British Government, which had told him that no help could be sent to him from Britain. In this royal order, there was no reference to the colonies; on the face of it, it ordered Danish subjects in the colonies also to submit.

Many people in those circumstances would have obeyed the order; to obey a royal command, whatever the circumstances, is usually the safest thing to do, especially for a colonial governor. But luckily for Denmark, and for America and Britain too, the governor of Greenland in 1940 was a man of independent character and some genius. His name is Eske Brun. It was obvious to him, as it was to everybody else, that the King had not given his command of his own free will; it was dictated by the Germans. But it was far from obvious at that time, just before and just after Dunkirk, whether this state of affairs was permanent, whether the Kingdom of Denmark would ever be free again, or whether, on the other hand, the governor of Greenland would always remain the representative of a King who was subject to German orders.

The constitution of Greenland directs that the country is to be administered in the best interests of the Greenlanders; and there is a clause in it which says that if communications with the mother country are interrupted, the administration should continue with this object in view. Strictly speaking, the German invasion did not interrupt communications. The Government in Copenhagen went on sending its orders to Eske Brun, by radio and through Portugal. But he decided he could regard the German domination itself as an interruption. It was something which stopped the true wishes of the King and Government from being sent to him. He decided to put the interests of Greenlanders first, to carry out the orders of the Government if he thought they were constitutional, and if he did not, to regard them as having been sent to him under duress. He decided, in short, to act as he thought the King would have wanted him to act if he had been free. With this decision, Eske Brun became the independent ruler of 22,000 people and of the largest island in the world. If declarations of war had not been out of fashion, Eske Brun would have felt inclined to declare war on Germany.

The governor was a civil servant, not a soldier; in fact, there was nobody with any military training in the whole of Greenland. But when he surveyed his domain from his capital at Godthaab on the west coast, he made several strategical guesses which all turned out to be right. The first was that although the war at that moment was being fought across the English Channel, Britain would hold out and America would come into it in the end; and that when she did, Greenland would have some importance in her strategy. He foresaw that the Americans would want air bases along his west coast, as stepping stones on the shortest route from America to Europe. Up until then, the Danish Government had not allowed anyone to go to Greenland without individual permission, because it wanted to protect the Eskimos from exploitation. But he saw that this policy would have to be relaxed. Greenland was sure to be drawn into the currents of world affairs, and to be influenced by strangers. All he could do was to try to make sure that the influence was harmless.

He also wondered what interest the Germans might take in Greenland. The very fact that he had defied them made it seem all the more likely that they would come there sooner or later. Certainly the west coast, the civilised and populated side, was quite safe from raids or landings: the sea and the air on that side of Greenland were firmly under American control. But on the wild east coast, there was nothing whatever to stop the Germans landing, except the British Navy, which had more than enough to do.

Eske Brun, without a single soldier, or any weapon more dangerous than a hunting rifle, could hardly think of defending his 1600 miles of vulnerable coast; but he did very much dislike the idea that anyone might invade it, and even establish themselves and stay there for years without ever being seen.

He consulted the Americans about this problem. They were not yet at war, but they were interested in the possibility of a German foothold in Greenland: for if Greenland could be a stepping stone to Europe, it could equally be a stepping stone from Europe to America. But in fact, the mechanised power of America could not do much to protect the east coast of Greenland: at least, not at a reasonable cost. In July and August, patrol ships could be sent rather more than half-way up it, at some risk of being caught in the ice and having to winter there. From spring to autumn, a colossal organisation at vast expense could have patrolled it with aircraft. But in the winter, when there are months of continual darkness, not even aircraft could have detected anything.

The Americans' first reaction to the problem was to ask Eske Brun to order everybody who was already on the northern half of the coast to come south to the settlement at Scoresby Sound. They pointed out that the coast would be easier to patrol if it was know to be totally uninhabited, so that anyone who was found there could be treated as an enemy on sight. After some hesitation, he agreed.

It turned out that at that moment, scattered along the 700 miles of coast beyond Scoresby Sound, there was a total of 26 men and one woman. There were twelve hunters, some Danish and some Norwegian. Each of them had a definite hunting district about sixty miles square, and lived in a hut in the middle of it. Each of them lived alone, except the one man who had his wife with him. These men very seldom saw one another, and only communicated once a year with the world outside. Besides the hunters, there were three Danish weather stations, which had radio transmitters, and one Norwegian one, and each of them had a staff of three or four men. The governor had to tell the Americans that the Norwegian Government in London was the only authority which could move the Norwegian hunters, because they had a treaty right to hunt there; but in the end, by radio through the weather stations, the order was sent out and gradually reached the most distant of the hunting districts; and in the course of the summer, all the hunters unwillingly drifted in to the weather stations or to Scoresby Sound.

It had certainly been the governor's duty to ask the advice of the Americans, as experts in large-scale logistics, about this problem of guarding the eastern coast; but he was probably secretly glad when he found they could not think of any easy answer. It was a matter of personal pride to him, and of political wisdom, to prove that Greenland could look after itself with the least possible help from any foreign power. So from the contemplation of fleets of ships and aircraft and armies of support, his thoughts turned to the couple of dozen men who were gathering at Scoresby Sound. The contrast was absurd.

Yet when he thought it over, it seemed paradoxical but less absurd. Possibly, he thought, in the extraordinary conditions of the arctic, a few men who had lived there before could really do more than an army and a navy and an air force. Certainly, they could not prevent a landing, unless it was a very small affair; but they might be able to detect it, so that he could tell the Americans where it was. Anyhow, he had invited the Americans to patrol his coast, and they had hesitated; and so, being the man he was, he offered to try it himself, and they gladly agreed. By radio to Scoresby Sound, he asked for volunteers, and chose fifteen. He called them the North-East Greenland Sledge Patrol; and as their headquarters, because it was near the middle of their beat, he selected the wooden house at Eskimoness.

4

THE SEVEN men who had wintered at Eskimoness were members of the sledge patrol; the other eight members were stationed at Ella Island, two hundred miles to the south, and at Scoresby Sound, a hundred and fifty miles farther still. Each of the men had a sledge and a team of dogs; and their assignment from Eske Brun was to patrol the coast from just south of Scoresby Sound up to the farthest limit which is ever navigable, that is to say from 70 to 77 degrees north. As the crow flies, their beat was 500 miles long. If anyone had the patience to measure the length of the coastline they had to patrol, along each of the fjords and round each of the islands, it might be ten thousand miles. But it did not seem to them an unreasonable task. Some of them thought it was quite unnecessary, but none of them thought it was difficult.

Even the ones who thought Eske Brun was wasting the Government's money had been glad enough to accept the job. It gave them a chance to go on doing what they had done before the war, to live the life they enjoyed, and be paid for it. All of them except two had been hunters, and to patrol the whole coast gave them excellent opportunities for hunting on the way. As hunters, they had lived alone in primitive uncomfortable huts, and their living had been precarious. Now, they could hunt almost as much as before, and yet they had an assured income, plenty to eat and drink, and an almost luxurious home in which they could rest between their expeditions.

Luxurious was not too strong a word for Eskimoness, by the standards of the arctic. It was a single-story, red-painted house with a large living-room in the middle. Six bedrooms, a radio room and a battery and generator compartment opened off three sides of the living-room, and store-rooms were built against the outer walls of the bedrooms; so that the house was in three concentric layers which sheltered and insulated each other and could all be heated by a big stove in the middle. It had been comfortably furnished in the modern style by the Danish Government.

Besides the main house, there were several outhouses which were used for storing coal, reserve provisions, dog food, paraffin, and petrol for the radio generators, and there was a little hut in which the hunters cured and stored their fox furs and musk-ox and polar bear skins. All the buildings, and the radio masts and a flag pole on which the Danish flag was flown, were scattered on a small patch of level stony land between the mountains and the sea.

The whole of the north-east coast is beautiful, all the hundreds and hundreds of miles of it; and the tiny part of it which could be seen from the window of the living-room at Eskimoness was typical of it all. Eskimoness is on the south side of an island called Clavering Island, about the shape and size of the Isle of Wight. The house was fifty yards from the shore, and from its window one looked out across a wide open bay to the mountains of the great headland with the curious name of Hold With Hope. From season to season, everything in this prospect alters, except the outline of the mountains. Within the few weeks of the summer, in July and August, the waters of the bay are blue, the mountains brown and grey except for the snow on their summits and the glaciers among them which never melt away. At that time of the year, it is something like a mountainous coast in the temperate parts of the world, the west coasts of Scotland or Norway, for example; except that all through the summer, from right to left, from the great glaciers out of sight at the head of the bay, a stately procession of icebergs drifts slowly towards the open sea. The sea in summer sparkles, and waves break on the shore; it is a scene with sound and movement.

The sea freezes quite suddenly in the autumn, and very quickly the scene is immobilised and silenced. Whatever icebergs are passing at that moment are frozen in, and become part of the landscape. After this, the foreshore is always white with snow, and the edge of the sea is only distinguished by the broken tumbled ice along the tide-mark. Beyond it, the same whiteness stretches as far as the distant land, which is also white except where the rock is too steep for the snow to lie. There is no movement then, except the movement of the sky, and no sound except the sound of the wind. No water moves, no insects hum, no plants wave in the wind; the birds have gone, the animals are seldom to be seen; the landscape looks like a silent still photograph of itself. This is the more familiar aspect of the view from Eskimoness, because it lasts so much longer, more than ten months instead of less than two.

In the days when people lived at Eskimoness, there was only one time in each year when the perfect peace of the scene was broken by any sign of civilised human life; and that was when the store ship was sighted, in the last week of July or the first of August, bringing the year's supplies. The supplies were always landed in a hurry, because the captain was more or less anxious about the condition of the drift-ice out at sea. For about three months in the year, everybody in the arctic, in places like Eskimoness, looks forward to the sighting of the ship. For two or three days, life is full of bustle and disturbance, of letters to be answered and jobs to be done against time; all the petty worries of the civilised world intrude. Afterwards, for several weeks, everyone is glad the ship has gone.

In the summer of 1942, the supplies had been brought to Eskimoness by an American coast guard ice-breaker. When it had gone, and the unaccustomed noise had died away and the mess had been tidied up, Eskimoness returned to itself again, and the sledge patrol settled in for the winter. For the moment, there was no patrolling to be done. During the summer, the men had moved around to a limited extent by motor boat, hunting seals and doing a little fishing, and laying depots of dog food and fuel at different places on the coast for use on their winter journeys. But in the autumn, when they were waiting for the sea to freeze, it was impossible to venture far by boat, for fear of being frozen in and losing the boat; and after the first freeze-up, there was longer to wait before the sea-ice was bearing and the sledge journeys could begin.

These men, waiting to be frozen in for a winter together, were a mixed collection, assembled by chance; but in spite of their differences in background and education, they got on well together, because all of them were bewitched by the arctic. The leader was a Dane called Poulsen. He was s slightly built, quiet, self-contained young man, the son of a bookseller in a Danish provincial town. There was no arctic tradition in his family; only coincidence had brought him where he was. After he had finished his apprenticeship in bookshops and had started to help his father, he had gone for a ski-ing holiday in Norway, and there he had met the secretary of the Danish explorer and geologist, Dr. Lauge Koch. Some latent spirit of adventure had made him ask Dr. Koch for a temporary job in Greenland the following year, by way of a long summer holiday from the book trade; and that summer had been enough to infect him with the arctic fever. He never went back to bookselling.

When the Germans invaded Denmark, Poulsen had been at home on leave. Like most young Danes, he wanted to get out of the country, so that he could do something active instead of passively putting up with the German occupation; but unlike most of them, he discovered a way of doing it. By then he had spent four years in north-east Greenland, mostly as a radio operator in the service of Count Eigil Knuth, another of the great men of Danish arctic exploration. Count Knuth had an arctic station of his own, one of the four stations in north-east Greenland which broadcast daily weather observations. By an extraordinary oversight, even in the summer of 1940, after the invasion of Denmark and after Dunkirk, all these stations were still transmitting in plain international code, simply because nobody had told them to stop. Observations from Greenland are very important in making forecasts of Atlantic weather, and accurate forecasts were equally important to both sides in the battle between German submarines and British convoys. Anybody could pick up the north-east Greenland broadcasts, and the British seemed not to have thought of supplying the stations with secret codes, and nobody in Denmark could send them a signal without the Germans' consent.

The men at Count Knuth's station were due for relief. Poulsen and he discussed the situation; and then the Count applied to the Germans for permission to send Poulsen and two other men from Denmark, on the German side of the battlefront, to Greenland, which had declared itself for Britain. Of course, the Germans wanted this free gift of weather information to go on as long as possible, and so they agreed to allow a small ship to sail from Norway to Greenland: probably the only time in the war that a ship left Europe with German permission to make for a country which was on the British side. Before Poulsen sailed, the Count gave him private instructions to stop the transmissions the moment he got to the station; but Poulsen did not need to be told. Provided with formidable passes, he and his two companions crossed the closed frontiers from Denmark to neutral Sweden and from Sweden to occupied Norway. In Ålesund, they joined a Norwegian sealer and sailed up the coast to Tromsö, where they left German waters, with German approval, for the edge of the arctic ice. The ship was supposed to bring back the men who were being relieved; but nobody on board it had the least intention of coming back at all.

Off the coast of Greenland, the sealer was intercepted by a free Norwegian gunboat under British orders, but when Poulsen explained what he was doing there, the ship was set free again. She could not reach Count Knuth's station, which was in 77° north, because the ice did not open that summer; but once Poulsen was clear of German control he was able to send a radio signal which stopped the uncyphered broadcasts, and in the following winter he reached the station by sledge. He was still there when Eske Brun gave the order for everybody to come south. So this bookseller became the leader of the sledge patrol.

Poulsen took his command very seriously. He was a serious-minded man; and certainly his position gave him plenty to worry about. For one thing, he was the only man at Eskimoness who believed there might ever be anything in north-east Greenland to interest the Germans, and that the sledge patrol might be anything more than a whim of Eske Brun's. He did not expect a real invasion; but his years as a radio operator had taught him the value of weather forecasts. When he had cut off the international broadcasts, he had known it would make a serious gap in the German weather maps. That was why he had done it. He could imagine that the German navy or air force might try to do something to fill the gap again. In the previous summer, in fact, a small German party with weather recording instruments had landed in Greenland, and had been rounded up almost at once by an American coast guard cutter. But Poulsen found it difficult to explain the danger to his hunters. They had made a bargain with Eske Brun, and they were quite willing to carry it out, but nothing could quite persuade them that it was not a lot of nonsense.

In those early days at Eskimoness, while they were waiting for the winter night to fall, Poulsen might well have wondered what he would do if the men he was supposed to command just refused to do what he told them. Nobody ever had a more isolated command, or a more tenuous authority. He had never met Eske Brun, who was quite inaccessible on the other side of the ice-cap. He had no uniform or military status: nothing but a radio telegram in code to say that a sledge patrol was established and that he was the head of it. If anything went wrong, there was nobody he could ask for advice, except by radio and in cypher; and if anyone turned quarrelsome or mutinous, or got seriously ill or went mad, there was nothing he could do but make the best of it on the spot. Once the summer ship had gone, there was no way out of Eskimoness except by a sledge journey of 400 miles to Scoresby Sound, and there was no way out of Scoresby Sound at all.

But perhaps the most formidable of all his responsibilities was that at the age of thirty-two, he was solely in charge of a hundred thousand square miles of Denmark's colony. This was no sinecure. In the 1930s, Norway had challenged Denmark's ownership of north-east Greenland. The case had gone to the International Court and had been decided in Denmark's favour; but countries, like individuals, may feel a sense of embarrassment at winning an argument with a close friend, and the Danes still felt like that about north-east Greenland. Eske Brun knew, and Poulsen had a shrewd idea, that there were plenty of Norwegians in Canada and England who would have been glad to come to take care of that part of Greenland; but that made it all the more important for Danes to prove they could look after it themselves. Otherwise the Norwegians would have a good reason to state their claims again. It must have been generations since such a young man as Poulsen had such a heavy colonial responsibility.

Poulsen's two companions on his strange journey from Denmark had followed him into the sledge patrol and were with him at

Eskimoness: Kurt Olsen and Marius Jensen. Kurt Olsen was almost a boy. He was only seventeen when they left Denmark, and hardly fully grown. After he left school, he had trained as a radio operator; and he had applied to Count Knuth for a job simply to get away from the German occupation. He had thought that if he did not like Greenland he could go on farther west, to America perhaps, to join an air force; but the arctic had absorbed him into its charmed circle, as it absorbs almost everyone. Poulsen had taken him on his winter journey up to Count Knuth's station, and taught him to drive dogs; and nobody who has been admitted to that mystery is ever quite the same again. So Kurt Olsen stayed, and finished his growing up, both physically and mentally, under Poulsen's tuition in the arctic. It was not a bad schooling. He had left Denmark timid and shy; but by the time the sledge patrol had assembled at Eskimoness, he was a tough handsome young man who impressed the old hunters as never being afraid of anything; and Eske Brun had appointed him second-in-command.

The third of the men who had travelled from Denmark, Marius Jensen, was a man of about thirty who had been a hunter before the war. In those days, two companies, one Danish and one Norwegian, had organised the hunting of fox and polar bear in north-east Greenland, and guaranteed the hunters a minimum wage. Marius had joined the Danish company and gone to Greenland for the simplest of reasons: he was hard up and out of a job. Like Poulsen, he was slightly built; and he was also extremely reserved and never talked unless he had something to talk about. Perhaps these superficial qualities were the only ones which Poulsen and he had originally had in common, because Poulsen's upbringing had been bookish and academic, while Marius came of country stock and was a farmer in his instincts; but by the time they came to Eskimoness there was something much more important between them: the unspoken brotherhood which unites men in the arctic.

This brotherhood is not a sentimental fiction, it is real. It is not very often put into words by anyone in the arctic, because, for one reason, it is so generally accepted that there is no need to talk about it. But looking back, one can see that it was the most important influence in all the extraordinary events at Eskimoness, so that unless one understands it one cannot entirely understand why the men who got caught up in those events behaved as they did.

The fact is that in the arctic men have a higher standard of morality than they have in civilised surroundings. Standards of morality are partly matters of custom and convention. In commerce, for example, one man expects another to bargain to his own advantage; in urban life, there are social ladders to be climbed; in employment, there is competition for promotion. All these aspects of civilisation are competitive and selfish; circumstances and conventions tempt every man to try to go one better than his neighbour, even though this may mean depriving his neighbour of whatever advancement both of them are seeking. Usually, this universal struggle and competition is silent and polite, and it sis so wholly accepted that one forgets that it is selfish; but it has the seeds in it of jealousy and covetousness and greed, and thence of crime.

Convention in the arctic is different. There is nothing to struggle for there, except to keep alive in difficult surroundings, and in this all men are in co-operation, never in competition; and so mutual distrust has almost died away. There is no crime worth mentioning in the arctic, except in the areas where civilisation has invaded it with air bases or mining camps or intensive trading in furs; and those places have ceased to be truly arctic. Nobody in the real arctic ever locks a door. It is taken for granted that any traveller will be welcomed wherever he may go: he may walk into anybody's house and stay there, whether the owner is at home or away. Even the poorest hut is left ready to be lived in, with a fire laid in the stove, in case somebody passes that way and suddenly needs refuge in a storm. It goes without saying that any man may look for help and kindness and generosity from any other. Political and social quarrels seem infinitely far away and quite absurd, and nobody takes much account of nationality.

Besides this, the arctic scene has qualities which bring out the best in every man. Nobody who has ever lived there for long has remained unmoved by its harmony and beauty. Even the least sensitive of men, alone in the arctic, feels nearer to whatever God he worships. Every man, within his limitations, becomes a philosopher. So the arctic paradox arises: that although a man can only live there by ruthless hunting, and although he must be physically tough, his relations with other men are gentle and trustful and peculiarly innocent.

None of the men at Eskimoness, except perhaps Poulsen, had analysed these ideas or even been more than half conscious of them in that winter of 1942; but when it came to giving some explanation, long afterwards, of what they had done and why they had done it, they all put thoughts of this kind into words of their own. By then, they were in civilisation again, and could look back on what happened with detachment; but in the meantime, at Eskimoness, the eccentricities of arctic behaviour seemed normal to them, and it was the rest of the world which seemed crazy.

5

WITH THESE traditions, the winter passed pleasantly at Eskimoness. If Poulsen had had misgivings, they turned out to be unfounded. The hunters were reasonably conscientious in carrying out the job which they had scoffed at, and when they were back at the house in between their patrols, their company was cheerful.

It is sometimes said that the polar winter night is depressing: stories are told of men it has driven mad. But if one can make any general statement about it at all, one can only say that to winter in the arctic accentuates some of the qualities a man already has. An unstable person without any spiritual resources of his own might find the darkness and silence either frightening or boring, but luckily that kind of person seldom goes there. On the other hand, it is certainly true that many people have profited by wintering there, rather as a religious person may profit by a period of retreat. For the rest of their lives, they value their recollections of its peace and freedom, and even when age has made them far too feeble, they still long to winter there again.

At Eskimoness, the sun is seen for the last time about the end of October. After that, around the middle of each day, there is a sunrise glow in the sky above the mountains of Hold With Hope; but each day the glow becomes less, and in December, even on clear days, it is hardly discernible. The sun rises again at the beginning of February.

But to say it is dark for three months does not mean one can never see. Falling or driven snow very often blots out the view, but when the weather is clear there is starlight or moonlight or the light of the aurora, and the gleaming white country reflects all the light there is. The distant mountains across the ice are sharply outlined in their pattern of black and white, and they seem much nearer and smaller than they are. There is no colour at all in the night-lit landscape: the moon shadows on the ice are grey: even the Eskimoness house looked grey in winter, so that in the spring when the sun rose again it was quite a surprise to remember the house was red.

Certainly nobody felt depressed at Eskimoness that winter, and afterwards they all looked back on the dark time as a happy and peaceful period of their lives, not only in contrast to life at home in Denmark, but also in contrast to the hectic events which followed in the spring. Life in the house was comfortable and companionable, and pleasantly free from most of the restrictions and annoyances of civilisation. But it still had one restriction: it was bound by the clock. Besides patrolling the coast, the men had been given the job of weather reporting, and they had to make observations and encode them and transmit them every six hours. Furthermore, one man was appointed to cook for the others, and he was entitled to let them go hungry if they did not get up in time for breakfast. This defeated one refinement of personal freedom peculiar to polar regions, namely that for half the year it does not matter at all what time of day it is. In the months of winter when it is dark all day, and the months of summer when it is light all night, there is no need to go to bed at night or to get up in the morning, no need to be tied to a cycle of twenty-four hours. A man who is travelling or living by himself can sleep when he is tired and eat when he is hungry, whatever his clock may say, and he can work when he feels inclined; and that gives him a constant and pleasant reminder that he is absolutely his own master.

For the sake of this feeling of complete freedom, all of them looked forward, after a week or so of comfort, to going out on patrol again. The hunters were away most of the time, but Poulsen and Kurt Olsen were more or less tied to the house because they were the only radio operators. They envied the others when they watched them go. There is something irresistibly exciting in driving a dog sledge out across the sea-ice in the starlight. Perhaps it is partly because the dogs are so excited. To work in a team is a Greenland dog's delight, the whole aim of its existence; and when it sees its driver beginning to load his sledge it gets just as excited as an ordinary dog which knows it is going to be taken for a walk. At Eskimoness, there were sixty or seventy dogs, not counting the puppies, when all the men were at home, because each of them had a team of eight or ten. Greenland dogs do not bark quite like other dogs, they howl when they are pleased; and whenever a sledge was made ready and one team was put to harness, all the others picketed round the buildings howled together with anticipation. It is the most arctic of sounds, and the most exhilarating and thrilling: a sound of infectious impatience for the first uncontrollable dash across the shore-ice and out and away to unknown lands and unpredictable adventures. When dogs have been rested there is no holding them, and often a driver had to anchor the sledge to a stake or a building while the traces are fastened one by one. Then, as soon as the last of the team is in place, and before they can mix up their traces or let off their spirits by fighting, he slips the anchor rope and jumps on the sledge as the dogs spring forward. For a few hundred yards the dogs gallop, until their first exuberance wears off and they settle down to the steady haul, away into the darkness, the lighted windows of the house glowing far behind, the sledge runners hissing on snow or rumbling with a deep bass echo on the hard ice.

Driving a sledge is hard work. It is seldom the driver can ride on the sledge and do nothing, unless he is following an old sledge track and the going is good and his journey is short. One reason, of course, is that it is always much too cold to sit still. Another is that the extra weight of a man slows down the team. A third is that although at a distance the ice which covers the fjords looks perfectly smooth, it is often a maze of almost invisible ridges, and ripples of hard wind-blown snow, and the sledge has to be helped and steered across them. On clear ice or hard snow, the driver usually skis alongside the sledge with one hand on the raised handle at the back of it. In soft snow, the dogs sink in to their bellies, and the driver may have to ski ahead to make them a track.

A dog team is driven by four words of command and a 25-foot sealskin whip. Of course a team can be trained to be driven in any language, but the Eskimo words of command are most often used in Greenland, because, go, stop, right and left, in the Greenland Eskimo language, are words evolved especially for dogs to understand. The signal to go or to hurry is an urgent "ah, ah", just like the bark of a dog. To stop is a more soothing long-drawn "ai". Right is a high-pitched, quickly repeated "illi, illi, illi". Left is "yu, yu". Right and left are backed by a crack of the whip on the opposite side to the way the team is supposed to turn; but a good team, and especially one with a good leader dog, respond to the words at once. If they do not, it is not because they do not understand them, but because sledge dogs always have wills of their own.

Apart from these cracks of the whip, a good driver seldom has to use it, and unless he is skilful it is generally thought to be best not to use it at all. If a dog misbehaves very badly, he should give it a flick of the whip on the top of its hindquarters. But with a 25-foot whip and ten dogs, it is not very easy to do. To hit the dog in the wrong place might injure it, and to hit the wrong dog is an insult and bad for discipline; and to hit oneself on the back of the head is easy but annoying. So in most drivers' hands the main use of the whip is simply that the dogs know it is there.

It is surprising that this archaic kind of transport, which Eskimos have used since before the beginning of history, should still have been the best kind in 1943; but so it was. There are machines which can travel on the ice, and if the Greenland government had had any, they might have been better for moving a lot of men or a lot of stores; but for one or two men to travel long distances, dog teams were still the most efficient and economical of all. Any kind of machine needs an organisation, to supply it with fuel and keep it in working order; but a Greenland dog does not need anything which is provided by nature on the Greenland coast, and it never breaks down. One dog can pull a weight of about 80 pounds: 800 pounds for a ten-dog team. Their speed depends very much on the weight of the load and the state of the ice. With a light sledge on hard ice, they are said to be able to gallop at 25 miles an hour for a short distance, for example when they scent a polar bear; but with a normal load on a long journey, allowing for days when blizzards stop them moving, 15 to 20 miles a day is an average, and 40 miles is a good day's run.

But dogs do much more for a traveller than merely drag his property along: they help him to hunt, and keep him company and protect him. Without dogs it would be dangerous to sleep in a tent on the ice, because of the polar bears which are fierce and inquisitive, and sometimes because of wolves. A sleeping man might not hear a bear before it attacked him, but a sleeping dog is always more alert.

The job of the sledge patrol was not merely to travel, but to search the coast for strangers, and in that, the dogs were more effective than the men. In fact, there were two reasons why the men had tackled the job with so little misgiving; and one of them was that they knew the dogs would do most of it for them. Sledge dogs are very intelligent, and even more inquisitive than bears, and they have a good sense of smell. Down wind, they can scent a man or a bear, or a hut that is lived in, two or three miles away, and they will always make towards the scent, unless the driver can stop them, to see what is going on. The men by themselves, especially in winter, could never have looked into all the small valleys where huts or tents might be hidden; but with dogs, all they had to do was to drive along off-shore, and rely on the dogs to smell out an enemy.

The second reason why the job was not impossible was that to live in the arctic, one is almost bound to hunt, and to hunt one must move around; and nobody can move there without leaving tracks. On the sea-ice, the snow is seldom thick: the wind blows it away as soon as it has fallen. But a sledge or skis, or even a pair of boots, compress the snow so that it cannot blow away. Fresh tracks appear as hollows in the snow, but after a wind the loose snow collects in drifts and the tracks in wind-blown places are left as iron-hard raised ridges which often stand where they are until the spring. So the patrols did not look for human figures or for huts: they looked for tracks, and for the pricking of the dogs' ears and the raised muzzles which showed there was something of interest in the wind.

By that winter, the men in the sledge patrol knew as much about dog driving and arctic living as has ever been learned by anyone except an Eskimo, and they kept up their patrol all through the winter. This is the time when arctic expeditions retire to their base camps, or even to arm-chairs in travellers' clubs in cities; the Eskimos themselves keep close to their winter houses. Generally, in the dark time, there is between 40 to 90 degrees of frost, and appalling blizzards tear down from the ice-cap to the sea. It is usually thought to be too dangerous to travel. But it can be done, if the traveller is prepared to live as simply as Eskimos have lived for centuries, and if he is always methodical and never careless. All that he needs is a tent, two primus stoves, a sleeping-bag and groundsheet of reindeer skin, and a rifle—besides, of course, his sledge and skis and experience and good health. With this primitive equipment the patrol men sometimes journeyed for two months away from Eskimoness.

Usually, they slept in huts. Before the war and Eske Brun's order had put an end to ordinary hunting, each hunter had had a fairly elaborate hut where he lived. This living hut was called a hunting station. But also, scattered through his district, he had a lot of smaller huts where he could spend a single night when he was going round his trap lines. These were spaced about twelve miles apart, a day's march for a man who was working traps. A lot of them were only six feet square, like a packing case with a stove in it, and they were mostly built of driftwood which had come down Siberian rivers and drifted right across the arctic in the ice. So the whole of the shore-line up to the neighbourhood of 76° north has hunting stations at intervals of about sixty miles, and hunting huts spread out between them. Every single hut is marked on the map of Greenland, so that at first glace it has a deceptively populous appearance; but the hunting huts, as opposed to the stations, were never inhabited. In 1943, all the stations were deserted, but the stations and some of the huts were still stocked with coal and driftwood, and in some the patrol had laid depots of dog food and paraffin.

But they could never depend entirely on the huts. Sometimes they were caught by blizzards in between them, and had to camp; and some of them really preferred their own tent on the pure clean ice to the huts, which at best had the vestiges of years of human occupation. In an arctic blizzard one mistake or one careless act is likely to be fatal; but if a traveller pitches his tent in time, before the wind rises so high that he cannot do it, and if he pitches it in a sensible place and builds a snow wall on the windward side of it, he can live in it in warmth and tolerable comfort however hard and long the storm may blow. Most of the possible disasters of the arctic have happened before, and warnings of them have been handed down from one traveller to another. A traveller pitches his tent on the sea-ice in preference to the land because there is less drift of snow; but he keeps it away from the shore-line where the tide breaks up the ice, and away from high cliffs or icebergs. By experience, he builds a snow wall just high enough to let a few inches of snow lie on top of the tent, to insulate it and stop the canvas flapping. He uses one primus stove for cooking, and another one for heating. He carries matches and primus prickers in a very safe place of their own, such as a bag on a string round his neck, because a man once nearly lost his life by losing his primus pricker. He takes everything he possesses inside the tent with him, except the sledge and the heavy equipment to which the tent is anchored, because anything left outside is apt to be blown away or buried or eaten by his dogs. He keeps his rifle underneath his groundsheet where it stays frozen, because otherwise moisture condenses on it and as soon as he takes it outside again its mechanism jams with ice.

These tricks of the trade, and a great many others like them, were everyday matters to the men in the sledge patrol, but they never neglected them through over-confidence. Only one of them had a serious accident that winter. He got carbon monoxide poisoning from the stove in a disused hut, and had to lie there alone for a fortnight, very sick, before he had strength to get up and go on with his patrol.

As for the dogs, they are born in the snow and live out of doors all their lives, and they never suffer from cold. In blizzards they curl up and let the snow drift over them, only keeping the tips of their noses out. Down there out of the wind, their thick fur keeps them warm, and they do not want to come out even to eat till the blizzard is over. They are arctic animals, perfectly adapted to their climate.

The seven men on their tremendous winter journeys were physically isolated by hundreds of miles of utterly barren mountains; but perhaps their mental isolation was even more complete. This was the winter of Stalingrad, North Africa, Russian convoys, air raids on

England, talk of the second front. Poulsen at Eskimoness used to hear of these things on his radio; but the men out alone on their sledges never heard of them at all. Sometimes when they came back to their base he remembered to tell them some odds and ends of news about the war, but there were always more immediate things to talk about. For them, there was no reality in world events. In some of the huts there were magazines and newspapers, either lying around or stuck on the walls to keep out draughts. Those were the only things they ever read, and their only reminder of the world outside; and most of them were more than ten years old.

So they travelled as if they were in a dream. One must picture each of them ski-ing beside his sledge on the vast expanses of frozen fjord below the dark loom of mountains which have never been explored, the only moving thing in the ice-bound starlit landscape; the rumble of the sledge, the panting of the dogs, an occasional call from the man or a crack of the whip breaking a whole winter's silence. When they lay out through blizzards in their tents, they were wholly preoccupied with the details of keeping alive. In the huts, when the weather was still, the dogs howling outside in the crackling frost were their only companions, ten individual likeable personalities. They talked to the dogs because there was nobody else to talk to. The things which occupied their thoughts, the true realities, had nothing to do with war: they were only the weather, the dogs, and the hunting; hunting for food for themselves and the dogs and for fox furs and bear skins which one day they might be able to sell. They never quite forgot that they were there to search for other human beings; but as the winter passed they could not believe they would ever meet anyone in that beautiful wilderness, or that if they did, the strangers would not be as friendly as all men had always been in north-east Greenland. But in that they were wrong.

PART TWO

SABINE ISLAND

6

THE GERMAN trawler *Sachsen* had sailed from Kiel in the summer of 1942. The sailing was a very secret affair, under direct orders of naval headquarters in Berlin. The ship had 19 men on board. Her captain was a man called Ritter, a reserve lieutenant in the German Navy, and besides her crew, she carried a doctor, two radio operators and a team of meteorologists. When Poulsen and Count Knuth between them had put an end to the international weather reports, it had made a gap, as they expected, in the Germans' forecasts: and the *Sachsen*'s mission was to fill the gap again. By 1942, in fact, the German need for weather reports from Greenland had become far more urgent than the Danes could have foreseen, because Russia was in the war, and the British had started their convoys to the Russian arctic ports. Submarine warfare and long-range air reconnaissance had spread north from the Atlantic to the arctic, and the convoys were being helped and the Germans hindered by the lack of German weather observations. A lot depended on the voyage of the *Sachsen*. She sailed past Copenhagen and up the coasts of Sweden and Norway all the way to Tromsö, where she left the shelter of the land, like Poulsen's boat two years before, and crossed the arctic convoy route alone.

For Lieutenant Ritter, this voyage in the middle of the war was something like a homecoming. Ritter was a man of fifty, graying a little, very tall and thin and aquiline, and he was not a German; or to be accurate, he was only a German by a chance of politics. He was born an Austrian, and had fought with Austrian alpine troops in the first world war. Some of his forebears were Scandinavian. But his birthplace was in the part of the Austrian Empire which became Czechoslovakian after the war was over, and so he found himself a Czechoslovakian subject. Then, in 1938, when the Germans invaded Czechoslovakia, his nationality was changed again, through no wish of his own. This time, he was simply told he was a German.

By then, Ritter had had several jobs, mostly as an officer in merchant ships of various nationalities and as captain in antarctic whalers. About 1913 he had been on the Prince of Monaco's yacht on a cruise to Spitzbergen; and Ritter was yet another man who had fallen in love at first sight with the arctic. He had seen something there which appealed to him intensely, in contrast to the web of the politics of central Europe, and he had never forgotten it; and in 1931 he cut loose from Europe altogether, and went back to Spitzbergen and lived there humbly for five years as a hunter. Those had been the only perfectly happy and carefree years he could remember since his childhood.

He had been delighted to be given command of the *Sachsen*: an appointment which would take him back to the arctic, not as a mere hunter but as a naval officer. As it happened, the appointment had also saved him from a difficult situation. He had been captain of a naval auxiliary vessel running between the North Sea and the Baltic ports behind the Russian front; but he had suddenly been removed from his command and sent ashore by the Gestapo. Nor charge had been made, and he did not know why he was under suspicion; a good many people knew he was not a Nazi, but he had always done his duty as an officer. Nobody had ever told him what went on behind the scenes, but it seemed to him afterwards that the navy had backed him up, and that they had defied the Gestapo by quickly finding him a new command which would take him out of harm's way. After a few weeks with nothing to do, they had appointed him to one of two ships which were to sail from St. Lazaire in France to try to reach Japan. The first of the ships was sunk just out of port by the Royal Air Force, and his own was recalled, and the trip was cancelled. He was not sorry. Luckily, discussion was just beginning of plans for the *Sachsen*'s voyage, and Ritter, a naval officer who had been an arctic hunter, was an obvious choice as her commander. Japan had been far away from the arm of the Gestapo: the *Sachsen*'s objective seemed even farther. Neither of them offered much prospect of getting back to Germany before the war was won. The whole incident had been a small example, curious to look back upon, of the division of German political and naval power.

As the *Sachsen* steamed north-west towards the ice, Ritter was happy to think he had left all that trouble behind him and had been given a job which he could do better than anyone else in the German Navy. The Gestapo affair had scared him, not for himself so much as for his wife and his only daughter. At best, Gestapo suspicion might have meant the loss of his livelihood, and hardship for them; at worst, it might possibly have meant that they would be arrested. But he had hopes of making a great success of the *Sachsen*, to show his gratitude to the navy and to prove, once and for all, that whatever the Gestapo might have thought, he was a good naval officer. His orders left him plenty of discretion, and they were so simple they could be put in a single sentence: to establish the meteorological party ashore in north-east Greenland. It was left to him to choose a place. If he could get his ship out of the ice again after the landing, he was to come home; if not, he was to winter there himself. To be on the safe side, he had taken two years' provisions.

In early August, the *Sachsen* reached the edge of the ice with Spitzbergen far to starboard and Iceland to port, and Ritter turned her westward along it, to keep as far as possible out of the way of British ships. He gave orders to lower her masts to make her less conspicuous.

The sight of the ice brought back so many memories to him that he could not bear to keep them to himself. He was the only man on board who knew the arctic, and the others were eager to listen to everything he could tell them. He poured out his recollections of his years in Spitzbergen, of the Scandinavian hunters he had met, the winter his wife had spent with him up there, the adventures and the freedom and peace and beauty of it all. Seeing the arctic again, he felt again the kind of love which has to be imparted: the same feeling which had made him persuade his wife, years before, to come up and join him, and stay there till in the end she learned to love it too. He confided most in the senior meteorologist, Dr. Weiss, and the expedition's doctor, whose name was Sensse, and in another member of the party called Schmidt, who seemed to have an educated background. Back in Germany, he had been worried about Schmidt, because he was a keen Nazi party member. He had felt that Nazism would be out of place in an arctic camp, and that Schmidt might be a difficult companion in the winter. He had even mentioned his doubts about him to the admiral who had given him his orders; but the admiral had said he was not responsible for the appointment and had told him to make the best of it. Now, in his own excitement at returning, his doubts seemed unfounded. He wanted to welcome Schmidt and all the others into the community of the arctic, and to watch the beginning of their appreciation of it.

None of these Germans had ever been to Greenland, not even Ritter, and nobody in Germany knew very much about it. They had been given some excellent Danish maps, taken from Copenhagen, and in July, Dr. Weiss had flown over the north-east coast in a Focke-Wulf reconnaissance aircraft from Norway. On that flight they had specially looked at the meteorological stations which were marked on the maps. At Ella Island they had not seen any sign of life, but at Eskimoness the Danish flag was flying, so they knew somebody was living there. Apart from that, they had very little information, and some of it dated back to a German expedition of 1870. None of them knew whether the coast was patrolled or guarded, or whether the Americans were there.

Technically, it was even doubtful whether the coast they were approaching was enemy territory or not. Germany did not consider herself at war with Denmark. Officially, German troops were in Denmark to protect the Danes against attacks from England. Ritter knew that the Governor of Greenland was in league with the Americans and British, and he was too intelligent to believe that Denmark wanted to be protected; but for all he knew, any Danes who were still in north-east Greenland might be cut off from the Greenland government. They might even be waiting for a chance to obey the King's order to submit to German occupation; they might be glad to see him. But he had no intention of meeting them to find out. That was not his job.

As the *Sachsen* crept westward along the ice, in the fine clear weather of August, her crew reckoned they had a slender chance of ever reaching Greenland. The British patrolled the channel north of Iceland: it was there that the battleship *Bismarck* had been intercepted the year before. A small ship being hunted in a hostile sea feels very conspicuous to the people who are on board it; but in a ship which is hunting, one is more aware of the vastness of the ocean and the smallness of anything sailing on it. Probably the *Sachsen* was in much less danger than they thought. Anyhow, nobody saw her. She passed well north of Iceland, and then turned farther north to penetrate the ice before she closed the coast of Greenland. On the 26th August,

Ritter sighted land. It was the southern point of Shannon Island, in 75° north latitude.

He had hoped to go farther north than that, because he believed that the farther north he went the less likely he was to be detected; but between Shannon Island and the mainland he saw an unbroken mass of solid polar ice. He pointed it out to the scientists, and said: "That's the end of the journey." Already it was late in the year. He ran a risk of getting the *Sachsen* frozen in before the meteorologists had been landed; and if she had stuck in the drift ice it would have carried her helplessly southward until, in the end, it crushed her. So he turned south, determined to land wherever he could find a sheltered anchorage. The first point he approached was Sabine Island, and there he saw open water close inshore. On the north-east corner of this island, there is a tiny fjord called Hansa Bay. It was free of ice. He turned the *Sachsen*'s bow towards it, and steamed slowly in. In the middle of the bay, she ran aground.

7

SABINE ISLAND was not a place which Ritter would have chosen if the ice had not forced him there. For one thing, it was too near Eskimoness, the only place on the whole of the coast which he knew was inhabited. It is only 70 miles away: a next-door neighbour, as distances are reckoned in the arctic. But in fact it was a very lucky choice. He was protected there by one thing he could not possibly have foreseen: it was notorious as a bad hunting ground, and so the men of the Sledge Patrol never went there unless they had to.

While the *Sachsen* was still feeling her way into Hansa Bay, something totally unexpected happened: the lookout saw an aircraft. It was flying straight towards them out of the north. For a moment, they thought it must be German, but then they saw it was a small single-engined flying boat. It came in on a steady course, almost as if it was running in to bomb them, and the thought came into Ritter's mind that his approach to Greenland had been too easy, that he must have been observed all the time and lured into an ambush. But the plane passed overhead, and disappeared to the southward, giving no sign that its crew had even noticed the ship in the entrance to Hansa Bay.

Long afterwards, the coincidence of dates and times proved that this aircraft was one sent out on reconnaissance by the American coast guard ship which, at that very moment, was landing the year's supplies at Eskimoness. It had been sent to observe the ice conditions, not to look for ships: but the fact that its crew flew right over the *Sachsen* without seeing her was an example of the difficulty of patrolling the coast by aircraft. Among the confusing lights and shadows of icebergs and innumerable dark uncharted rocks, even a ship is difficult to see: a hut or a tent on the shore would be quite invisible, even before the snow put its camouflage over everything. The episode gave Ritter and his men a sense of security, although they could not imagine where the aircraft had come from.

They floated the *Sachsen* again without much trouble, and anchored her farther in near the head of the bay. But on their way north, in a storm, one of their lifeboats had been smashed, and with only one boat left it was clearly going to take a long time to get all the meteorologists' gear ashore. Anyhow, the freeze-up was imminent. To make a thorough job, Ritter could only wait till the ship was frozen in, and then land in comfort across the ice. Besides that, the radio transmitter which the meteorologists had brought turned out to be inadequate, so the ship's transmitter had to be used to transmit the weather reports. Ritter was glad to have such good excuses to winter there, and not to take the *Sachsen* straight back to Germany.

In the meantime they covered the ship with white camouflage sheets to make it look like an iceberg, and began to explore Sabine Island and make plans to defend it. The island is nine miles square. The mountains round there are not high, but they are steep. The island itself has several flat-topped hills about two thousand feet high, and Hansa Bay is surrounded by them. There are two huts on the island: one is a very small hunting hut in Hansa Bay itself, and the other an old Danish hunting station on the south end of the island, near a small bay appropriately called Germania Harbour.

The geographical names on the north-east coast are a mixture of nationalities, English, Scottish, Norwegian and Danish, Dutch, German and Austrian, and, in one part, French. They have all been bestowed by members of the successive expeditions which have partially explored the coast. The peninsula of Hold With Hope was named by Hudson, who sailed round it in 1607, much the earliest of all the explorers there. A Scottish whaler, Captain Scoresby, discovered Scoresby Sound in 1820, but the Eskimo colony there, which now bears his name, was only established thirty years ago. The first organised expedition was an English one in 1823, under Captain Clavering, who gave his name to the island on which Eskimoness stands. The Sabine of Sabine Island was the leader of his scientific party. A German expedition wintered in Germania Harbour in 1869, and called the little anchorage by the name of their ship; and since then, many explorers have found tracts of unnamed land and taken the opportunity to immortalise themselves or flatter their protectors. Some of the names are so unattractive that one must suppose they served financial ends. A vast and beautiful stretch of water, for example, is called Kaiser Franz Joseph Fjord; and on the south side of it is Geographical Society Island. Other names suggest a pathetic nostalgia for home, like the rock which rises from the middle of a glacier and is marked on the Danish maps as Scotstounhill, or the great fjord opposite Eskimoness which is called Loch Fyne. Many places have women's names, like Ella Island and its neighbours Maria Island and Ruth's Island, and the barren stretch of ice which is called Miss Boyd's Land. It is still possible to achieve this particular kind of immortality. One of the hunters in the sledge patrol was a man named Henry Rudi, and the stretch of water in front of the hut where he lived is marked for ever on the maps as Rudi's Bay.

Hansa Bay is another German name from 1869. It is certain that of all the explorers who had ever seen the place before Ritter landed there, none had ever looked at it with an eye to military defence; but it was a good place from that unusual point of view. The steep hills protected it from the air, and in summer nobody could approach it except by climbing the mountains or by navigating slowly and carefully among the icebergs along the strait from which it opens. In winter, there were only two ways to get to it, from the north or the south across the open ice; and the northern side would have been a difficult approach, because where the polar current strikes the island it piles up a mass of pressure ice. Anyone coming across the ice would be at the mercy of even a single sentry with a machine-gun in a prepared position. But in any case, there was no question of an armed attack at all so long as nobody knew the Germans were there. Ritter's first line of defence was simply to lie low and avoid being seen, and that was easy. His ship froze in, and snow drifted over her till she was buried. The huts which were built on shore were buried too. By October, there was nothing to be seen in Hansa Bay except a slender radio mast, some mounds of snow which had not been there before, and within a small area between the mounds a network of human tracks. One would have had to be within a few hundred yards to see the base at all. But by then it was sending reports three times a day to the German Navy.

It is hard to say exactly when the trouble began up there on Sabine Island; but certainly from its earliest days, this was a much less happy camp than the one at Eskimoness. It was only to be expected that some of the Germans would be bored. With the whole of the *Sachsen's* crew, there were too many of them, and they did not have enough to do. As they had no dogs and no experience of winter travelling, they could not move away from their base, but were all cooped up in Hansa Bay together. They never had a chance to get the true taste of the arctic winter, which can only be savoured in solitude. Ritter knew that it was dangerous to let them roam around, not only because they might get into difficulties of their own, but because of the tracks which they would leave for any traveller to see, if there were any travellers; but after a time he had to take that risk, and let them go out for short distances towards the open sea to try to hunt for bears or seals, partly to provide fresh meat, but more in order to occupy their minds and give them some exercise.

But that was not a very serious trouble; far deeper was the difference between the characters of Ritter and of Schmidt. Ritter had been mistaken in hoping to enjoy the winter. At first, he went on naïvely confiding in Schmidt, expecting that as an educated man he would be friendly, and hoping that the prospect of living together through the winter would make Schmidt look for common ground. But Schmidt remained aloof; sometimes he even seemed hostile. Ritter began to believe that Schmidt felt himself frustrated. It seemed that he must have thought from the very beginning that the expedition should be commanded by a Nazi party member, not by the senior naval officer. Ritter concluded that he had been annoyed and disappointed when the *Sachsen* was frozen in, because if she had gone, he might have hoped to be left there in command.

Such feelings are a simple human failing which anyone can understand, and Ritter felt some sympathy for Schmidt; he himself had had disappointments of that kind, when he had been passed over for promotion, but he had learned to live them down. He redoubled his efforts to be friendly; and to make things easier for Schmidt he made a point of deferring to his wishes and those of the other Nazi party members. Some of them, for example, wanted to give a weekly political lecture to the men. Privately, Ritter thought it a ludicrous idea, but he agreed. Then, of course, he had to attend the lectures, and to give the impression of endorsing what they propounded. They were embarrassing occasions. Ritter had heard it all before; but suddenly, hearing it again in the arctic night which had meant so much to him, the doctrine of Nazism doubly nauseated him.

During the winter, he fell into the habit of spending a lot of his time alone in his cabin in the *Sachsen*, or walking about the sea-ice in the darkness, trying to recapture his old feeling for the arctic. The starlight, the aurora, all the cold beauty were the same, but he seemed to be out of touch with them. Before, he had been alone, but now he was in company, and although he liked a good many of his companions, some of them were so uncongenial and seemed so out of place in those surroundings that he had to make an effort of will to speak to them; and that ruined the peace of mind which had been his most valued memory of Spitzbergen. Ritter was a deeply religious man, a Catholic by birth and upbringing; and he was introspective, the sort of man who tries to consult his conscience before the smallest action. In his solitary years in Spitzbergen, although he was far away from any church, he had been more aware than ever before or since of the hand of God. Now, when he looked up at the mountains round Hansa Bay, so calm and immaculate, the political talk and warlike preparations seemed to profane them.

Most men could have turned away from these sombre doubts and flung themselves into practical activities to forget them; but it was Ritter's nature to torment himself by following his most disturbing thoughts to their logical conclusions. They soon brought him to a conclusion, or rather to a conflict, which must be most difficult for an officer of any armed force of any nation. The belief began to crystallise in his mind that his duty as an officer and his duty to God were two different things which could never be reconciled. Ritter was not a pacifist: he would gladly have fought to the death for a cause he believed in. In the first world war, he had fought with enthusiasm and conviction for the Austrian monarch. In this war, his conviction had never been whole-hearted, even at home in Germany; and now, the arctic had reminded him again of causes much older than patriotism and a creed which was deeper in his nature than any political creed. Slowly, all through that arctic night, a suspicion grew clearer and clearer in his mind: the simple suspicion that the German cause was wrong.

But luckily, for the time being, Ritter's only duty as an officer was to look after the men under his command. That was a human duty as well as a naval one; so far as that went, his conscience and his naval oath were in accord. For the rest, he put off making a decision, even in his own mind, and simply hoped that he would never be called on to do anything which his conscience would say was wrong.

It was after this, later in the winter, that Ritter first began to be afraid. It was only a trivial incident that started it. He had been sitting in his cabin reading a book about the arctic when some of his men had knocked on his door and come in. Looking at them, he realised that they were a Nazi deputation. When he put his book down, one of them picked it up and looked at the author's name and said: "You know this man is a Jew." Ritter shrugged his shoulders. He had not known it, but he could not pretend to care: the man had been fond of the arctic and had known a lot about it. They took the book away.

It was the sort of thing that Nazis often did, and it was not of much importance in itself; but it was the first time they had come out into the open to oppose him. The words "You know this man is a Jew" had not been a question, they had not invited the obvious excuse: they had been an accusation.

As Ritter pondered unhappily over this incident he was gradually overcome by a sickening sense of dread. All that time, he had thought he had left the Gestapo behind in Germany; but he began with horror to suspect that he had not. His suspicion leaped to Schmidt. Who was Schmidt? Had the Gestapo picked him by some roundabout means and planted him to keep an eye on the commander the Navy had appointed? It was not an unusual thing for them to do. Who was in league with him? Did he know about Ritter's own earlier trouble or not? Was he trying to turn the crew against their captain?

Ritter sat alone, uncertain whom he could trust, who were really his friends and who were secret enemies. He recalled conversations with Schmidt himself, with Dr. Sensse and Dr. Weiss and all the other expedition members. There was the first engineer, whose name was Nowotny. Nowotny was an Austrian by descent, like himself, and lived in Czechoslovakia. He was a man who seemed to appreciate the arctic stillness: he had lived in a tent on the sea-ice for weeks at a time, so that the others had started calling him the Czech Eskimo. Ritter remembered asking him if he was not worried about his family at home in Prague, because if Germany lost the war the Czechs would turn them out of the country. It had been a rash thing to say, even though Nowotny, like the others, had seemed to be a man after his own heart.

He remembered the dinner on Christmas Eve, when everyone had called on him to make a speech. Of course, he had spoken then of the message of the birth of Christ, of peace and goodwill; and even while he was speaking, and looking round at the faces of his companions at the table, he had known that some of them thought he should have spoken of victory rather than peace.

Above all, as fear grew to monstrous proportions in Ritter's heart, he thought bitterly back over the last few months, of all the confiding things he had said to Schmidt, all he had told him about the international friendship of the arctic, the gentle liberal conceptions he had tried to put into words, all the ideas which meant so much to him and, now that he came to think over them again, were so exactly the opposite of Nazism. Now that it was too late, he saw how unwise he had been to let his enthusiasm carry him away. Schmidt had just listened to it all and made no comment; but had he been carefully noting it down against him?

It was this impression that evidence was being collected against him which frightened Ritter. He was not afraid for himself: he had no exaggerated fear of death, or of anything the Nazis could do to him. But the old fear rose up again for his wife and daughter.

Every German officer knew that if he gave offence to the Nazi party, his family might be punished. Most of them never had any serious inclination to be disloyal to the party, and so they did not mind. It was not supposed to be a matter of justice; it was simply a threat, intended to keep the few waverers in order. But being deliberately unjust did not make it less effective; and although Schmidt was not a senior member of the expedition, Ritter knew perfectly well that Schmidt or any other Nazi would report him if he thought he had a case against him, because it was his duty to the Party.

As soon as Ritter had begun to realise what was going on, he made up his mind to be careful not to offend his Nazis any more, for the sake of his wife and child. He became much more sensitive to hostility which he had hardly noticed before: an insidious half-hidden hostility which was hard to pin down to any definite act. But a week or two later, something happened which proved he had left it too late to be careful. The doctor, Sensse, came in to his cabin.

"Ritter," he said, "I think you ought to know that some of the men are trying to send a telegram to Berlin to say you are not to be trusted."

The doctor went on to tell Ritter that so far as he knew, the telegram had not actually been sent. One of the Nazis, he said, had given it to the radio operator with instructions to send it without telling the captain. The radio operator, caught between two authorities, had asked the doctor for advice, and the doctor had decided that rightly or wrongly Ritter was in command and ought to be told about it. Ritter thanked him.

But when he was left alone again, more doubts and suspicions were added to the confusion in his mind. He had always like Dr. Sensse, and had never been able to believe he approved of the Nazi party. He was certainly intelligent and sensitive, and did not seem to be hypnotised by Nazism. He was a big strong man, who Ritter felt might have fitted well into his conception of arctic life. Ritter had always thought that if he and Sensse had been alone there as hunters, they would have got on very well; and now he had shown himself friendly by warning him about the telegram.

Yet Ritter could not question him more closely, or invite his sympathy. If he were really a Nazi, or were somehow under the influence of Schmidt, to say any more could only add to the terrible trouble which was brewing; and if he were not, there was the risk of compromising him in Nazi eyes. Thinking alone about the telegram, Ritter took it for granted that Schmidt was at the back of it; but he wondered if Schmidt had really meant the telegram to go. There did not seem to be much point in actually sending it, when all of them, whatever happened, were imprisoned together for another six months in Hansa Bay. It was hardly likely that Berlin would have acted on it, without any further inquiries, by taking his command away and promoting Schmidt as the senior party member, or Dr. Weiss as the senior scientist, or one of the officers of the *Sachsen*. But on the other hand, if Schmidt had not meant to send it but had planned, in some way or other, that the doctor should tell him about it, then the thing had a point. For one thing, it was a final warning to Ritter, a convenient way of telling him that the Nazi case against him was complete, that the Nazi faction was ready to act on it if necessary, and that therefore he had better do as he was told. And it was also a thing which could easily be twisted to Schmidt's advantage if it ever came to a court of inquiry. Ritter could imagine his evidence: "I attempted to report these matters, in accordance with my duty, but the captain suppressed the report."

At this point, Ritter might possibly have forced things to a showdown; but whenever he tried to plan what he ought to say to Schmidt, he came up against the most horrible thought of all: that the Nazis were legally right. Ritter could see their point of view, only too clearly; and he knew even better than they did the extent of the doubts in his mind. Schmidt, he reflected, like any young man, was not to blame for being a Nazi. Ritter was old enough to remember the world before Nazism, but Schmidt had probably been at school when Hitler came to power, and been carried away at an impressionable age by what had seemed in those days to be a new idealism. Even Ritter had seen the insidious attraction of Nazism, in spite of his deeper convictions. It was not the fault of Schmidt that Nazism had gone mad and run wild; and Ritter knew that once a young man was enmeshed in its mass beliefs, it was almost impossible for him to cut loose from them and begin to see its faults. Now, Schmidt suspected him of disloyalty to Nazism, and he was right. The difference was that for Schmidt, that meant disloyalty to Germany, and for Ritter it did not. Yet Ritter could only reflect that if the Nazis had really known all the half-traitorous thoughts in his mind, they would have come for him with a gun; and still he could not have blamed them.

By February, when the dark time ended and the tops of the northern hills were pink, and the sun could be seen again from the sea-ice outside the bay, and everyone should have been happy to think that the spring was coming, the German camp was confused by rival loyalties and distorted politics. Its commander was a lonely bewildered man, far lonelier than he had been in the years in Spitzbergen when he had been alone. He did not know who could be trusted or who were his enemies, and he dared not confide in anyone; and he was hounded by three conflicting forces. There was his naval duty; and that was still compelling, because he was grateful to the senior officers who had backed him against the Gestapo and entrusted him with an independent command, and because the Navy still represented Germany, and because he loathed the idea of being a traitor. There was his conscience, which had been brought to life again by the old influence of the arctic; and it was perfectly sincere, more the conscience of a monk than a naval officer. And sinister, at the back of all he did, was fear: the terrible haunting imagination of what the Nazis might cause to be done to his wife and daughter.

Nevertheless, for six continuous months, the German transmitter on Sabine Island had been sending out daily reports, unknown to the British or Americans, which were guiding German submarines and aircraft in their attacks on the arctic convoys.

PART THREE

THE ENCOUNTER

8

IT WAS about the beginning of March when Poulsen said to Marius Jensen, "You'd better have a look at Sabine Island."

This was the busiest time of the year for the sledge patrol. The worst of the winter storms and cold was over, and the daylight was rushing towards the equinox, increasing by twenty minutes every day from the darkness of early February to the midnight sun of early May. The spring is the most brilliant of the seasons in north-east Greenland. It is still very cold, and the thaw is still far away. There are no signs of budding life, the whole land remains motionless and silent: but it is deluged with light of superb intensity, and each mountain, the ice underfoot, each crystal of snow, glitters in blinding immaculate perfection.

It is in this cold flood of light, in March and April, that conditions are best for sledging. It is not too cold for the men or too hot for the dogs. In the hardest winter frost, the snow is as dry as sand and a

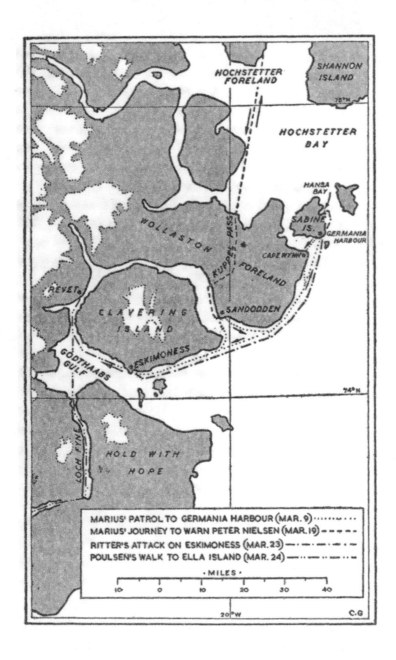

MARIUS' PATROL TO GERMANIA HARBOUR (MAR. 9) ·········
MARIUS' JOURNEY TO WARN PETER NIELSEN (MAR. 19) — — —
RITTER'S ATTACK ON ESKIMONESS (MAR. 23) — · — · — · —
POULSEN'S WALK TO ELLA ISLAND (MAR. 24) — ·· — ·· — ··

· MILES ·

Sledge Patrol's district: northern part

sledge does not slide on it easily; by May, the heat of the sun when it is high makes the snow sticky and distresses the dogs, and one has to travel in what is left of the night; and in June the thaw begins. So in March and April, Poulsen had planned to cover the whole of the coast and patrol all the places which for one reason or another had been inaccessible in the winter.

In those early days of March, all of the seven men except one were at home at Eskimoness but all of them except Poulsen were ready to start on journeys. The one who was away was a young hunter called Peter Nielsen. He had spent most of the winter alone in the district of Hochstetter Foreland, a hundred miles north of Eskimoness, and at the end of April he had gone even farther north to inspect the coast up there and to hunt for dog food. Marius Jensen was to go north with the two Eskimos who had wintered at Eskimoness, to take three sledge loads of stores up to Hochstetter Foreland and meet Peter Nielsen there; and it was on this journey that Poulsen suggested he should make a detour to Sabine Island.

Marius did not want to go to the island. "You know it's a hopeless place for hunting," he said to Poulsen. "And the weather's bad out there. There's nothing but fog at this time of year."

Poulsen reminded him that the object of the patrol was not really hunting, it was to make sure there were no Germans around; and he pointed out that none of them had been to Sabine Island for nearly a year. But Marius was mildly annoyed at being reminded. "That's not the point," was his argument. "The point is that even if the Germans did come to north-east Greenland they wouldn't choose a place with bad weather and bad hunting." But he knew Poulsen too well to expect him to change his mind. It was only a token protest. On March 8th, he started on his journey.

The two Eskimos who went with Marius were called William and Mikael. They were both young men from the colony at Scoresby Sound, and the fact that they both had European names is due to the curious history of the east-coast Eskimos. As they drove out on that March morning from Eskimoness, they passed a historic spot called Dead Man's Bay. It is full of the ancient Eskimo graves and ruins which are found here and there all over the north-east coast; and there, though they may not have known it, the first encounter took place between a European and a man of their race.

That was in 1830, when Captain Clavering anchored there. On shore, he found six people, living in a skin tent. They were simple and very primitive, but friendly. For two or three days he tried to talk to them, and he offered them food and asked them on board his ship. It is recorded that he had one of them washed, to find out what colour his skin was. They did not object to that, but on the next day he showed one of them a pistol and invited him to fire it. The Eskimo pulled the trigger, the pistol went off, and all six of them fled into the hills. They were not only never seen again, but no living Eskimo was ever discovered after that on the north-east coast; those six in 1830 had been almost the last of a race which was dying out.

However, in 1886 a colony of them was discovered at Angmagssalik, eight hundred miles farther south. There were 416 of them alive. They had never had any contact whatever with civilisation and were living in the Stone Age, and they also were on the verge of extinction from starvation. But the Danish Government took them in hand, fed them, gave them modern hunting weapons in place of their stone-tipped spears, and taught them Christianity. As a result, their numbers increased in the next fifty years from 416 to over 1500; and they and their descendants turned out to have an unexpected degree of native intelligence. By the 1920s there were so many of them round Angmagssalik that the local hunting grounds could not support them, and it was then that the settlement at Scoresby Sound was founded. Eighty volunteers from Angmagssalik were moved up to Scoresby Sound, and by 1942, in their next generation, they numbered 200.

Of these, there were six in the sledge patrol, two who remained at Scoresby Sound, two at Ella Island and two at Eskimoness. They were intelligent sensible people, expert hunters and devout Christians. They could all read their own language. But of course their view of the world was rather limited. None of them had ever been away from the coast of seen a city bigger than Scoresby Sound, or met anyone except their own relations, a few hunters and Danes in Government service, and possibly one or two members of arctic expeditions. Like all Eskimos, they were perfectly peaceable, easy-going and friendly. The idea of great nations at war was very difficult indeed for them to grasp. To meet a hostile man was just as unlikely, in their experience, as to meet a friendly bear.

Because of this natural and possibly enviable limitation, and as a matter of policy, Eske Brun had only allowed the Eskimos to be enrolled in the sledge patrol as assistants, to drive sledges and hunt, and lay depots of food. The Danish aim in Greenland had always been to protect the Eskimos from the worst aspects of civilisation and to preserve their best characteristics. The war had become a Danish war, but it was certainly not an Eskimo war; and Eske Brun, from the very beginning, had decided never to let Eskimos be involved in anything so unnatural to them as warfare. So the Eskimos in the sledge patrol were not asked to patrol alone; and if anyone ever seriously thought about fighting, it was generally understood that the Eskimos would be kept out of it.

On their first day out of Eskimoness, Marius, William and Mikael made their way along the south side of Clavering Island and round its south-east corner, to an old hunting station called Sandodden, which stands on the shore of Wollaston Foreland, facing the island across Young Sound. So far, Marius was in familiar country, because the usual sledge track to the north goes up Young Sound and then crosses Wollaston Foreland by a low col called the Kuppel Pass, a few miles beyond Sandodden. Sandodden was one of the hunting stations which the patrol had used fairly often, because it was a good first day's journey from Eskimoness, a matter of 30 miles. There was quite a substantial house there, with two rooms and a sleeping loft. It was notable for being liberally decorated inside with hunting scenes in poker work.

Each of the men was using a team of eight or nine, and their sledges were more heavily loaded than usual because of the extra stores they were taking up north to Peter Nielsen. At Sandodden, where they spent the night, it was a temptation to go straight on over the Kuppel Pass, instead of going the long way round the outside of Wollaston Foreland and Sabine Island. Apart from the weather and the hunting, there was another bad thing about Sabine Island, especially for people with heavy sledges: and that was that just south of it is one of the worst stretches of ice on the coast. The current from the north makes an eddy round the south side of the island which breaks up the ice from time to time all through the winter. There may be leads of open water at any time of year, and there are always pressure ridges where the ice has broken and buckled; so it is always a dangerous difficult place to pass. That night at Sandodden, they all grumbled more or less about Poulsen's way of taking the whole patrol so seriously, but Marius had promised him he would try it, so that was that. The next day, they started the trek along the south-east coast of the Foreland.

The Greenland air in early spring is perfectly dry and clear, and visibility is so tremendous that a visitor from a dirtier, damper climate is given a totally false impression of size and distance. Normally, unless there is a fog produced by some local disturbance, one can see at least 120 miles; and when one looks at mountains across the ice which are twenty or thirty miles away, it is sometimes hard to believe they are more than four or five. One result of this deceptive appearance, even to a seasoned traveller, is that one seems to travel desperately slowly: hours and hours, or even days, of hard going on sledge and skis make very little difference to the landscape.

It was nothing unusual, therefore, that Marius and his companions could see Sabine Island right in front of them two days before they got there. The last twenty miles of the coast of Wollaston Foreland are a straight line of basalt cliffs only broken by one large valley, and Sabine Island sticks out beyond the end of them. All through the first of those two days, the view in front of the sledges, beyond the fan of dogs, changed very little. To the left were the cliffs, very black in contrast to everything else; above them a glimpse here and there of the ice-covered hills, and below them the broken masses of the shore-ice. To the right, the ice stretched to a sharp horizon, interrupted by ridges of pressure and icebergs frozen in, gleaming with iridescent colours against the sky. The cliffs tapered in perspective to the far distance, and there, perfectly clear but in miniature, were the flat-topped hill of the island. Behind them, and out of sight, was Hansa Bay. To Marius Jensen's knowledge no human being had set eyes on this scene since August the year before.

As the tree men and the twenty-five dogs went on, all their thoughts were on a single subject: bears. The defect of Sabine Island as a hunting ground was that there were usually no herds of musk-ox to be found there; but there were bears. The musk-ox, a comparatively slow and harmless animal, is the main source of food for travellers and their dogs. It looks like a small buffalo, stands about four feet high, and is very good to eat; and as its only natural enemy is the wolf, its only idea of self defence is to run to the top of the nearest hill and there form a square, back to back with the rest of its herd, like early infantry. Therefore there is nothing exciting about shooting a musk-ox; but a bear is a very different thing. Hunting a polar bear from a sledge is breathlessly exciting and fairly dangerous, and a bearskin is worth quite a lot of money, and a traveller may meet a bear at any minute on the outer coast, even round Sabine Island. This possibility shortens the longest journey.

All three of the men were keeping their eyes open as they drove along, partly in the hope of a hunt, but especially because when two or three men are together, the skin of a bear belongs to the first man who sees it, not to the man who eventually shoots it. Besides, it is an advantage to see a bear before the dogs scent it and get excited, because then the hunter can make preparations in peace. He unloads the sledge and dumps everything he possesses on the ice, except his hunting knife and rifle. Then he calls to the team to go—"Ah, ah"—and cracks his whip and jumps on the sledge as the dogs take up the pull. By then, the dogs know there is something up, and they sniff the wind and hurry. The bear can move fast, and nobody can tell what he will do. The hunter can only guess, and direct the dogs with "yu" and "illi". But when they pick up the scent, they take up the hunt themselves. The sledge then sings across the ice. It is very low, and the driver is close to the ice, and 25 miles an hour seems a tremendous speed: the wind of it stings the eyes, the dogs yell, the driver holds on and shouts "Ah, ah", not because it is needed by simply because he must.

A bear hunt is never the same twice, and it needs judgment to succeed and to avoid disaster. At a crucial exactly chosen moment, the hunter slips half his dogs from their traces, to leap ahead and bring the bear to bay. The dogs cannot kill the bear, but the bear can kill the dogs. Yet most dogs will attack without any hesitation. If the hunter slips them too soon, the bear may catch one or two with a blow of its paw which can instantly kill a dog or a man stone dead, and the others may take up a running fight which will draw away from the sledge which is moving more slowly with only half the team. But if the hunter waits too long before he slips them, the bear may turn and get among the dogs while they are hampered by their traces, and then, laying about it, it can kill a lot in a split second before the hunter can get a clear shot.

The hunter's own life, of course, depends on his rifle, but in bear hunting by daylight the main dangers for him are indirect, the dangers of breaking a leg or losing his dogs a very long way from home. In the dark, a bear hunt is perhaps even more exciting, and certainly more dangerous. Then the dogs scent the quarry first, and the hunter does not know what he is hunting till he sees it or sees its tracks. It may be one bear or more, or a musk-ox, or a fox or even an arctic hare, which can easily outrun a dog. If it is a bear, the added danger is that a bear is amazingly skilful at moving on thin ice, and will make for a patch of thin ice if he can find one; and a sledge at full speed in the dark cannot stop. Sometimes hunters disappear and are never heard of again; and one of the likely guesses about their fate is that they followed a bear in the dark and drove at full speed onto thin ice and fell through, hunter and dogs and sledge and all.

In the dark, the quarry is sometimes surprising. Once in the winter, when Poulsen and the Dane from Scoresby Sound were on patrol, their dogs scented game, and they unloaded their sledges and gave the dogs their head. They galloped inshore towards an iceberg and went round it at full speed, one sledge on each side, the men riding their sledges with rifles cocked and ready. On the other side of the iceberg, looking rather alarmed, was Peter Nielsen, who they had thought was hundreds of miles away.

In the patrol at Eskimoness, they had one of the arctic's greatest experts on bear-hunting. He was the only Norwegian there, and his name was Henry Rudi. He was a much older man than the others, in his middle fifties, and he had lived in the arctic for most of his life. He was said to have shot more polar bears than any man alive: something in the neighbourhood of a thousand. Naturally, there was not very much that this veteran did not know about the arctic; but most of his time had been spent in Spitzbergen, where dogs are not so widely used, and most of his bear-hunting had been done by spring-guns and other nefarious means; and one of the pleasures of Eskimoness that winter had been to pull Henry Rudi's leg about his driving. It is always a test of a driver's control to stop his team when they see or scent something ahead which interests them. It was said that Henry Rudi had given up trying to order his dogs to stop, and the others earnestly advised him to adopt the idea of another well-known hunter, who carried a boat's anchor on his sledge which he cast overboard whenever the dogs ran away with him: a practical plan which struck the patrol as uproariously funny. Luckily, Rudi was one of those cheerful endearing people who seem to enjoy being laughed at. He had done a lot to enliven that winter with experiments in distilling, which were sometimes abortive but almost always festive, and with the stories which he told against himself, like the story, famous already in arctic circles, of how he once returned to Tromsö or some such civilised place with a world's record bag of 165 polar bear skins. On that heroic occasion, finding himself a very rich man, he had hired a whole hotel and invited every passer-by to come in and stay there as long as he like, with drinks on the house. At the end of a fortnight, he had had to go back to the arctic to start all over again and it took him another five years to get the same number of bear skins; but he said it had been very well worth it.

At Eskimoness, Rudi was on his home ground. For some years his hunting district had included most of the coasts of Clavering Island, and before he had joined the patrol he had lived in a hut he called Revet on the opposite side of the island. In those days, he used to visit Eskimoness, and before he left, it was a custom to ask him which way he meant to go home, right or left round the island: it was 35 miles one way, and 70 the other. He always avoided the question and changed the subject, and usually tried to start when nobody was looking; but everybody watched from under cover. He would cross the shore-ice calling "illi, illi", with a false air of confidence; but as he realised that once again his dogs had made up their own minds, his tone changed to exasperation and his language to Norwegian. "Right, blast you," the listeners would hear, "right, sons of Satan"; and Norwegian oaths would fade into the distance as his dogs carried him quickly away to the left.

However, bears like dogs are unpredictable creatures, and Marius and the two Eskimos, on their way towards Sabine Island, saw no sign of them. For the third night of that journey, Marius had decided to stay in the hunting station at Germania Harbour, on the south side of Sabine Island. They approached it across the sound which separates the island from the mainland, after a very hard day's driving. The ice for the last fifteen miles had lived up to its reputation. They had not seen any open water, but they had had to pick a way between the ridges and pinnacles of broken ice, and heave the sledges up and over the edges of piled-up floes. In some places the sea-ice had been so bad that they had crossed the shore-ice and driven along the land, which is a most unusual thing in Greenland. So the men and the dogs were tired.

In spite of the gloomy reputation of Sabine Island weather, it was still crystal clear and calm, and from right across the sound, five miles away, they could see the black speck of the hut at the foot of the Sabine hills. As they crossed, Mikael went off to the right to look at a skerry called Walrus Island which lies in the mouth of the sound. The dogs had been going slowly, and needed some urging to keep going at all.

About half-way across, Marius saw his dogs prick up their ears and lift their drooping tails. Something had roused them. Their pace began to quicken. Marius thought: a bear. He could not see anything, so he called his dogs to a halt and got out the field-glasses which he carried in a bag which was hung on the uprights of his sledge. He swept the horizon, searching for the slightly yellow speck which he hoped to see. But all he noticed was that Mikael, away to the right, had halted and was examining the ice.

His dogs were eager to move again, so he let them go, and they started to carry him straight on towards the distant hut. Marius was puzzled. The dogs were behaving just as they would have behaved if the hut had been lived in; but if Marius could be certain of anything, he was certain that nobody had lived in the hut for nearly a year;

and after so long it could not have carried any scent. He thought of a bear scavenging behind the hut out of sight. But Mikael had started his sledge again and was coming back towards him, so he stopped to wait and picked up his glasses again and focused them on the hut, and then he saw the quite incredible thing: in the still clear air, a small wisp of smoke from the chimney.

Marius stood there amazed. It was years since he had seen a track in the snow or a sign of life in a hut without knowing at once who had made it. Then the obvious explanation came into his head. There was only one man to the northward, and that was Peter Nielsen; so it must be Peter, who had come south for some reason or other to meet them. But that theory only lasted a moment. Mikael came dashing up, and he was shouting: footsteps—human footsteps—boots—boots with heels. Nobody Marius knew wore boots with heels, except ski boots, and nobody walked about in ski boots. Marius looked again towards the hut, and he saw two specks appear beyond it. Through the glasses they were two men, running: and they were not running towards him, they were running away. He stood still on the ice and watched them. They ran to the hills at the back of the hut and began to climb them. They went up and up without a pause, and when they got to the top they disappeared, over a col towards the middle of the island.

At this fantastic performance, Marius gave up trying to find an explanation. It had crossed his mind, just before he caught sight of the men, that if it was not Peter Nielsen a plane must have crashed in the district and some survivors have got to the hut. But why run away? And why, of all things, run up into the mountains, where nobody in Greenland ever goes unless he is following a musk-ox?

At the end of a hard day's driving in Greenland, if one sees a hut with smoke from its chimney, one drives thankfully up to it, giving a shout from some distance away so that the person inside the hut will put the kettle on. So, after they had got over their first surprise, Marius and the Eskimos drove up to the hut at Germania Harbour, and stopped their dogs on the shore below it, and walked to the door and went in.

There was nobody there. It was nice and warm inside. The stove was still alight, and there were two half-empty mugs of coffee on the table. Lying on one of the bunks, there were two daggers, and there was a jacket of an unfamiliar greenish colour hanging on a hook on the door. Marius looked at it, and on the breast of it he saw the swastika.

9

WHEN THE two hunters came breathlessly in from the outpost at Germania Harbour, Lieutenant Ritter was in bed with a temperature; but the news which they blurted out soon brought him to his feet.

The story they told him was so stupid from a military point of view that it was almost funny, but its possible implications were serious enough. If they had only waited in the hut, they could perfectly easily have shot the sledge drivers as they approached across the open ice, or ambushed them and taken them prisoner. But something of the arctic spirit had got into those two men. They had run away and come back to base, they explained, because they had not been able to bring themselves to shoot: and that curious explanation, which perhaps had never been offered before to a German officer, was one which Ritter could easily understand. Even Schmidt, when he was told, knew what they meant.

Anyhow, Ritter wasted no time on remonstration. The main question was whether they had been seen. They said they were afraid they probably had, as they climbed the mountain. Then Ritter knew he would have to act quickly and decisively, or his first line of defence would be gone. He guessed the three sledges had come from Eskimoness, simply because so far as he knew there was nowhere else they could have come from within three hundred miles. He took it for granted that Eskimoness had a radio transmitter. And therefore, if the three drivers, or even one of them, got back to Eskimoness alive, the Greenland government and the Americans and British would all know where his base was hidden.

It was five miles from the base at Hansa Bay to the hut at Germania Harbour. Five minutes after the two hunters came in, eight Germans set off, in two separate parties, armed with sub-machine guns, rifles and revolvers, with orders to get the three sledge drivers and bring them in, preferably alive, but if necessary dead. One of the parties was led by Ritter, who was still feeling ill, and the other by Dr. Weiss. Schmidt was in Dr. Weiss's party.

10

MARIUS JENSEN tried hard to explain to William and Mikael that the swastika was the sign of the enemy. They thought it was all very interesting and rather exciting. Neither of them knew what he meant.

All three of them poked about inside the hut and looked at the tracks outside it, and gradually Marius began to put two and two together. It is easy, looking back at the whole affair from a standpoint outside the arctic, to say that he was slow in his reactions. Afterwards, he said so himself. But for a roughly similar situation, one must imagine a New Yorker or a Londoner, in that same winter in the middle of the war, coming home after a hard day in the office to find a posse of German soldiers in his sitting-room, and to see them run away as he came up the garden path. It is really not surprising at all that Marius found the whole thing took a lot of believing.

However, when he had had a little time to get used to it all, the signs at the hut told a clear enough story. He could only find two sets of human tracks, and no sledge tracks. There was an uncured bear-skin and half a bear's carcass. There were two eiderdown sleeping-bags in the hut, the sort one might use in a base camp but not in a tent, and there was very little food or fuel. The equipment, so far as it went, was good, and did not have the makeshift look of having come out of a crashed aircraft. On the other hand, there was no traveling gear at all. Everything suggested a short hunting expedition from a base not far away; and when he came to think of the map, and the direction the men had taken in the hills, there was only one place that the base was likely to be, and that was in Hansa Bay.

Once he had come to this conclusion, Marius realised they could not hang about at Germania Harbour, and he told the two Eskimos to get ready to leave. "What, now?" was their reaction. "Not to-night?" They said they were tired, and so were the dogs. So was Marius, but he explained that they ought to get home to tell Poulsen as soon as they could, and besides, the enemy might come back; and after a while, they all agreed, and stirred up their unwilling teams and started to drive slowly back across the sound. It did no occur to any of them to take the swastika jacket or the German daggers. In the ethics of war, one talks of capturing booty; but in the arctic, war or no war, stealing was stealing.

Even at that stage, the things that really mattered to Marius were the things that always matter in the arctic: the state of the ice and the weather, and the welfare of the dogs. It was getting dark by then, and ahead of them was all the difficult ice they had crossed in the morn-ing. The dogs could have gone on: a good dog will go on till it dies if its driver tells it. But if a driver overtires his dogs on one day, they have much less strength than usual on the next; and if he overtires them badly, they may suffer the results of it for months. So this is a thing which a self-respecting driver never does: and the principles of good dog-driving were still more important to Marius than the principles of war. Eskimoness was sixty miles away. The dogs had to be rested somewhere, and the sooner the better. The first hunting hut on the way home was straight across the sound, on the point of the mainland which faces Germania Harbour. It is called Cape Wynn; and there Marius, William and Mikael decided to spend the night. None of them really had any idea that the information they possessed was about as dangerous to live with as a time-bomb.

The routine of a night stop is always the same. The sledges are unloaded, and everything is taken into the hut. The dogs are unharnessed and picketed on the long chains which are carried for the purpose, and then they are fed. Each man likes to feed his own dogs. Somebody lights the stove, and somebody gets snow to melt for coffee. As the hut warms up, the travelling clothes are taken off and hung in the roof of the hut to thaw and dry. Everything begins to steam comfortably. The meal at the end of the journey is the main one of the day: it may be tinned meat, or frozen musk-ox, or pemmican if things are getting short, with coffee, and butter and jam on some kind of biscuit, or bread, if one of the party had been baking.

After it, the sleeping-bag is overwhelmingly attractive; but the sledge patrol always had one other chore which Eske Brun had ordered, and that was to write a log of the day's journey. It bored them. But that night at Cape Wynn, Marius at last had something of interest to put into his log book, and after supper he settled down laboriously with a pencil.

It was midnight when the dogs began to howl.

11

WHEN RITTER got to Germania Harbour, it was getting dark, and Dr. Weiss had already arrived with his party and discovered there was nobody in the hut. Ritter was annoyed with himself. He had been quite fit all through the winter, and now, the first time something happened which really called for his leadership, he was ill. It was nothing serious, but he felt weak and dispirited.

There was no sign of strangers in the hut. Nothing had been touched. The whole thing might have been put down to imagination, except for the fact that down on the shore there were the clear tracks of several sledges.

In the feeble state of mind brought on by his illness, Ritter was inclined to think there was nothing more to be done. On the face of it, it was ridiculous to try to catch sledges by following them on foot. None of the Germans was equipped to go far, especially in the cold of the night. In particular, they were wearing leather boots instead of fur ones, which is one of the surest ways of getting frostbite. Logically, by all the arctic rules, to go on was to ask for trouble, and was very unlikely to do any good at all.

But Dr. Weiss, on the other hand, who knew much less about the dangers and had never seen a dog sledge, was eager to try to follow up the tracks, and he was supported by Schmidt and several of the others. Ritter knew that if anyone went, he ought to go himself, but even the five miles from Hansa Bay had taken a lot out of him, and he could not face the idea of going any farther. But he knew better than to argue, especially with Schmidt; so he reluctantly let them go. He stayed at the hut, and watched them set off like hounds on a trail, following the tracks across the sound.

They had not gone very far before they had the satisfaction of being proved right, for this simple reason: that from half-way across the sound they could see a light in the hut at Cape Wynn, where Marius and the Eskimos, in their innocence, had not thought of blacking out the window.

The men spread out in a quarter circle and crept very quietly towards the light. A full moon was shining above the steep hills behind the hut; but in the shadow of the hills, it was dark. They stumbled through the shore-ice. On the shore the snow squeaked under the leather soles of their boots. They heard dogs growling.

Suddenly the light went out. They all ran forward to converge at the place where the light had been, and the sound of the dogs turned to furious howls and they found themselves among what seemed a milling mass of dogs which leaped at them with bared teeth, snarling. In the darkness it was some seconds before they saw that the dogs were chained and that they could reach the hut by going round them. Weiss dashed for the door of the hut, ready for a desperate resistance, and jumped inside it. It was empty.

It was only a minute since the light had gone out. He knew the sledge drivers were there. He wasted seconds in searching the hut, and then ran outside again into the tangle of dogs in the darkness. He found the sledges. His men scattered, but to begin a search was hopeless, and knowing that his enemies were there, presumably armed, not more than a stone's throw away in the darkness, he could not risk using a light. He shouted to tell them to surrender; but the only answer was the snarling of the dogs.

Weiss was surprised and baffled. For the moment, the men had slipped out of his grasp, just when he had been certain he had caught them. But he still thought he had won the day, because although the men had gone, he had firmly captured the sledges and the dogs. When he looked round more closely, inside the hut and outside it, he was even more sure of himself, because he found three sets of fur clothes and boots and gloves. He knew how far it was to Eskimoness, and he reasoned that the three men would have to come back to get their equipment before they froze to death. He posted one of his men to look out for their return, and he and the others went into the hut to get warm. They were hungry, and there was white bread and a pot of marmalade laid out for them, and coffee on the stove. They were delighted to discover American cigarettes. They amused themselves by trying to read Marius' log book, which was lying open on the table. Confidently, they settled down to wait.

12

THAT WAS the Germans' only mistake; because Marius, William and Mikael never thought of going back to get their gear.

The howling of the dogs is a language which a sledge driver understands, and when the dogs started that night it was not a howl of pleasure or contentment, or a howl at the moon, it was alarm. The men jumped to their feet and made for the door, but one of them had the sense to blow out the lamp before the door was opened. Running out from the lamp-lit hut into the darkness, they could hardly see anything at all; but they heard the Germans coming across the shore-ice.

Everything happened in a few seconds. William and Mikael tried to harness the dogs. Marius saw it was too late. Their retreat by sledge was cut off by the Germans between them and the ice. Before even one of the dogs was in its harness, the Germans had rushed and stumbled into the midst of them, and the dogs were snapping and leaping against their chains. For a moment, the Germans and the sledge drivers were hardly an arm's length apart, with the dogs between them. Then Marius shouted in Eskimo to run for it, and all three of them ran round the hut and started to climb the hill.

Behind the hut, it goes up steeply for six hundred feet, but they fell and slid back in the drifts of snow, and they had not climbed very far before they were out of breath. They stopped to look back, but there was nothing to be seen. Even the hut was only a darker smudge against the snow. They had heard Weiss shouting, but they could not understand what he was saying. The Eskimos were urging Marius to come on, but he wanted to wait and collect his wits and see what was going to happen; so he whispered to them to go on without him, and get to Eskimoness if they could and tell Poulsen what they had found. They went, and left him alone.

While the Germans waited in the hut, and one of them stamped his feet on the sentry-go outside it, Marius was shivering behind a rock two hundred feet above them. The sudden attack, and especially the capture of his dogs, had made him see at last that the thing was serious. He hardly knew what he was waiting for. Perhaps he forlornly hoped that the Germans would go away, as he had gone away at Germania Harbour, and leave his property behind. But anyhow, he could not wait for long. As Weiss had surmised, he would soon have frozen to death with none of his outer clothes on; and besides, if they did not go, he would have to be well away by daylight, because he had no intention at all of being captured. After half an hour or so, he gave up hoping, and turned away from the hut and climbed the hill. Weiss, in the hut, had taken it for granted that nobody would try to walk to Eskimoness, with only half his clothes and no food at all; but, difficult though it might be, it never occurred to Marius to try to do anything else.

Round about two o'clock in the morning, he got to the top of the hill. On the other side of it, in the moonlight, range after range of white mountains could be seen, still standing in friendly solitude and silence. He was thankful to see them again, and to be out of sight of the human intrusion at Cape Wynn. He began to plough his way down the other side through waist deep snow; aiming to meet the shore again ten miles beyond the hut.

Marius and both of the Eskimos had taken their rifles with them when they ran so hurriedly out of the hut, not because they had any idea of shooting anyone, but because an arctic hunter picks up his rifle by instinct. It was lucky for Marius that even in the excitement his instinct worked; because in the dawn, almost as soon as he got on to the sea-ice again, he met a bear. Among the broken ice, he was almost on top of it before they saw each other. He stopped in his tracks and watched it; and it watched him.

One of the curious things about polar bears is that in nature they never see any animal which does not run away from them as well as it can; and so if a man stands his ground in front of a bear, or goes towards it, it often takes fright and goes away. But on the other hand, if the man runs away, the bear regards him as another animal, much easier than most as prey, and it will lope after him and almost casually fell him with its paw.

For once, Marius did not want to shoot the bear. He did not know how close the Germans were. They might easily have come along the sea-ice more quickly than he had come over the hill, and he thought they might hear a shot. So he advanced towards the bear, hoping to scare it; but it would not move. For some minutes, he and the bear stared each other out, each waiting for the other to give the first sign of fear. It was Marius whose nerve broke first: he reluctantly raised his rifle and fired. The bear fell dead. The sound of the shot echoed round the hills and he listened, half expecting shouts or an answering shot; but the silence fell back again.

Marius left the bear where it had fallen, and walked on in a daze of weariness. He had been tired the afternoon before when he got to

Germania Harbour, and the events of the night had been a strain on him. Now that he had lost his dogs and his log book and all his most precious possessions, he saw only too clearly how unwise he had been to underrate the Germans. He had never thought they would follow him to Cape Wynn, but they had, and now there was every reason to think they would follow him farther. Even if they had had no dogs before, they had them now, so there was nothing to stop them catching him up at any minute. There was even his own outgoing sledge track on the ice to guide them. For miles and miles, he kept looking back, expecting to see his own dogs coming up behind him, with Germans behind the sledges. His two Eskimos had disappeared, and anything might have happened to them. If the Germans caught him, the way was wide open for them to go on to Eskimoness and surprise his comrades there.

The thought of the unknown enemy behind him, and of his friends at Eskimoness all unsuspecting and unprepared, spurred Marius on. But already he had been on his feet for a night and a day, and travelled on skis and by sledge and on foot for nearly fifty miles, and his pace was falling; already, he was hungry; and still Eskimoness was fifty miles away.

13

ESKIMONESS WAS in one of its quiet periods; nearly everyone was away. Kurt Olsen, the young radio operator, was patrolling Hold With Hope, with an Eskimo whose name was Aparte, and Old Henry Rudi had gone, to the left this time, round Clavering Island. While Kurt Olsen was out sledging, Poulsen was doing the weather broadcast single-handed, and was also teaching the job to a man called Eli Knudsen. Knudsen had been in charge of the station at Ella Island all the winter. The patrol had a radio set down there, but there had been nobody there who could work it. Knudsen had managed to use it for telephony, but that was no good for secret signals, and both Poulsen and Kurt Olsen had had to go all the way to Ella during the winter to mend it. Four-hundred-mile sledge journeys to service a radio set were not a very economical arrangement, and so Knudsen had come north, in that early spring, for a few weeks' lessons in Morse and maintenance, and he had brought his two Eskimos with him.

The only other person round about Eskimoness on March 12th, was the fourth of the Eskimos. His name was Evald, and he was hunting in the district to build up the stocks of dog food, so he was in and out of the house from time to time.

Thus it happened that Poulsen himself was the only man at the house just then out of the seven who had wintered there, or used it as their winter base. For him, Eskimoness was more of a home than anywhere else in the world. He had lived there for two years, and collected the usual clutter of personal belongings which most men accumulate when they live in one place so long. For most of the last two months, he had lived alone. He had been quite content. It had been a busy, methodical life, and he liked method. The weather reports had to be sent every six hours, and it took him an hour to read the instruments and encode and transmit the readings, so his day was divided into four five-hour periods. In one of them he slept, and he dozed for a bit in another. The others were pleasantly filled up with domestic chores: cooking and baking and brewing beer, doing the washing and cleaning the house, digging away the snow from the doors and windows, and mending things like sledges, harness, clothes, boots, and the battery-charging plant and the radio. To him, it had seemed a perfectly satisfactory day-to-day life. He had never thought of getting bored. He knew he was lucky to be doing something in the middle of the war which suited his tastes so well, and he would not have changed jobs with anyone, except perhaps his hunters, or exchanged Eskimoness for any other home.

In the course of the winter, Poulsen's worries about his responsibilities had more or less calmed down. His authority was still as nebulous as ever, but nobody challenged it, and the hunters had cheerfully gone as far north as Dove Bay, 300 miles up the coast, and made sure there were no intruders there. In a few weeks' time, the patrols would have filled all the gaps which had had to be left in the winter. Poulsen was the sort of man who is much too conscientious ever to be complacent about anything he has done; but anyone else might have congratulated himself, by the end of the winter, on having made a fairly good job, in the face of all the difficulties, of ruling the 500-mile domain which had been put in his care.

It was 11 o'clock in the morning of March 13th when Poulsen looked out by habit across the ice and saw the sight which put a sudden end to the peace he had enjoyed all through the winter. It was only a dark speck that he saw, but he knew what it was even before he had reached for his field-glasses. It was one man, alone, about three miles away to the eastward, and he was walking. He shouted to Knudsen to harness a few dogs and go out to bring the man in, and he began himself to get things ready in the hut—the stove, the first-aid chest, hot drinks and a bunk—because a man without dogs, walking could only mean disaster.

He had imagined every possible disaster by the time the sledge came back. He went out as Knudsen came across the shore-ice, riding the sledge with an almost lifeless man lying on it: Marius.

"Germans," Knudsen shouted, "Germans at Sabine Island."

Poulsen felt a surge of excitement mixed up with anxiety: the patrol had been worth it after all, had done what it had been supposed to do. The sledge drew up and Knudsen jumped off it, and Poulsen ran to give Marius a hand: Marius, grey with exhaustion, tattered, dirty. He could only gasp out an incoherent story: the Germans were there and had got the sledges and might be coming any minute to attack. Poulsen and Knudsen hauled him up and helped him indoors and noticed he had lost his boots and had been walking in his socks. They worked over him and found he had nothing wrong except first-degree frostbite which would cure itself; and they warmed him up and gave him a drink and some food and put him to bed, and questioned him harshly because they had to know what had happened before he fell asleep.

As the story came out, it confirmed Poulsen's first reaction. The patrol had really done what Eske Brun had meant it to do: it had spotted a German landing. But so far it had only done half the job. The other half was to get the news out, to tell Eske Brun, so that he could tell the Americans and they could come with their unlimited forces to wipe the intrusion out.

The next radio schedule was due in half an hour, and the one after that was six hours later. From what Marius said, there seemed to be every chance that in less than six hours the Germans would be there at Eskimoness. The minute Poulsen had pieced the whole story together, he sat down and wrote a signal and began to work against time to put it into cypher. At midday, Scoresby Sound was on the air, and he started to send them his message for onward transmission to Eske Brun. The first half of the signal was sent at 1200. The second half had to wait till 1800, because he had not had time to encypher it. It was written in all the hurry and excitement, and did not exactly agree with what Marius remembered after he had recovered.

FROM ESKIMONESS

MARCH 13TH

TO BRUN GODTHAAB VIA SCORESBYSOUND

1500 March 11 Marius William Mikael arrived hut on Sabine Island. At 500 yards from hut observed two men one dog climbing west side of Germaniaberg. In hut found green uniform jacket with German eagle and swastika on sleeve plus two new sleeping-bags socks and gloves. No food equipment or fuel which suggest persons base is in neighbourhood. All three drove to Cape Wynn hut to stay overnight. 0050 heard strangers approaching hut whereupon Marius William Mikael hurriedly climbed mountain behind hut. From 600 yards distance Marius heard shouts but did not understand language. After waiting half an hour Marius decided abandon three sledges 25 dogs and travel equipment at hut and returned here on foot with Eskimos only bringing rifles. Logs and orders therefore also abandoned. Expecting Olsen back from Hold With Hope Wednesday. Unless otherwise ordered propose leave then for further reconnaissance. Request orders. POULSEN.

Between the transmission of the first and second halves of this signal, quite a lot had happened, and the second half had been re-written several times. William and Mikael had arrived, bedraggled and weary but otherwise not much the worse; and Poulsen had had time to make up his mind what to do. With so much to think about, nobody bothered to ask Marius how he had got back to Eskimoness, and afterwards, when they did ask him, he could hardly remember anything about it. The bare facts make his journey unique of its kind in arctic travel. At the end of a very long day, in which he had already travelled something like forty miles, at one o'clock in the morning of March 12th, he finally left Cape Wynn; and at 11 o'clock in the morning of March 13th, he was sighted from Eskimoness. In 34 hours, without any food whatever, he had climbed over the hills at the back of Cape Wynn and walked 56 miles across the ice. He had stopped once, so far as he could remember, at a hut where he had made a fruitless search for food; but that had been near the beginning, soon after he had shot the bear, and remembering how the smoke at Germania Harbour had given the Germans away, he had not dared to light a fire; so he had had to go on again before he got too cold. Somewhere on the way, he had passed William and Mikael, who had stopped in a hut and gone to sleep. Somewhere, his skin boots had fallen to pieces. But it always happens when a man drives himself to the very limit of endurance that his memory of his experience is dim, and nobody will ever know much more than that of the journey which Marius made.

Once Poulsen had got his signal away, he felt a bit happier, not only because he had done his job, but also because he supposed the

American Air Force would be getting under way and would take charge of the whole situation within a day or two. In the meantime, he had to prepare to hold on until they came; and his first idea was to collect as many men as he could at Eskimoness in case the Germans arrived there with evil intentions. That same afternoon, he went out on the ice to have a look towards the east. From a little way out beyond the house, one can see a very long way along the coast. With glasses, a sledge can be seen at twenty miles; and so far, there was nobody coming. So he took the risk of sending the only other able-bodied man, Eli Knudsen, round towards Henry Rudi's hut to try to find the old man and bring him back. There was nobody who could go to look for Kurt Olsen, and nobody knew exactly where he was, so nothing could be done about him; and Peter Nielsen was so far away up north that he would have to be left where he was for the moment. But when Marius had had his sleep out, and Knudsen and Rudi had come in, there would be four men, not counting the Eskimos; and Poulsen reckoned that when Kurt Olsen came back too, he could safely leave them all to look after themselves, and go alone to have a closer look at Sabine Island, unless the Americans had already come to bomb it.

During the same evening, two sledges were seen, but nobody was very much alarmed because they were approaching from the west. It was Knudsen and Henry Rudi, whom he had found more quickly than Poulsen had expected; Rudi was anxious and rather more subdued than usual. Poulsen explained the plan of defence which he had thought out, such as it was, and they all got down to work.

The first thing was a plan to retreat. They were not feeling defeatist, but they had no idea what they were up against, how many Germans there were, or what their intentions were, or what sort of weapons they had. They had an idea they might be attacked by air; and if anyone in the arctic were bombed out of his house, it would not just be a matter of taking shelter with a neighbour. So three of the four remaining dog teams were picketed some distance away from the house behind a hill Poulsen's own dogs were kept by the house as watchdogs for the night. A depot of tents and provisions and traveling gear was laid in the hills, so that if the worst came to the worst they would be able to get away to safety. All the patrol's written orders, accounts and telegrams were hidden in a hole in the rocks, and all the ciphers and codes except one were buried.

For the more active defence, they blacked out the windows and began to build breastworks of sandbags inside them; and bit by bit they put up firing points at strategic places round about the house, barricading them with sacks of coal and empty coal sacks filled with broken ice. That night, when it started to get dark, they took a last look along the coast, and then one man was set on watch outside the house. It was the first time such a thing had ever been necessary at Eskimoness, or anywhere else in Greenland.

In spite of all these warlike preparations, the men that night were in a divided state of mind. Poulsen did not even try to sleep. The trouble was that he did not really know if he was supposed to fight the Germans. He was only a civilian, and so were all his men; and he vaguely knew that civilians who took up arms against a soldier were breaking some curious international convention. Worse still, he had never actually seen a statement of the policy of the Government of Greenland. All he had been told to do was to try to find a German landing if there was one; and the general idea had always been that once it was found, the Americans would deal with it. To look for Germans was a different thing from shooting them. Personally, Poulsen was not yet in a frame of mind for shooting anyone. If the Germans really came and tried to break up his home, he certainly meant to stop them if he could; but even a warlike person would hesitate to shoot when he was not quite certain whether his Government was at war, whether his shooting would earn him a medal or a charge of murder. All in all, Poulsen was very glad when the morning of the 14th came, and the sea-ice was as desolate as ever.

But Poulsen was luckier than many men who have been left in charge of distant outposts. In Eske Brun he had a commander who knew his own mind and could guess what was going on in the minds of his subordinates. The next morning, an enormously long signal came from the west coast; and as Poulsen ploughed through it with his cypher book his spirits rose.

TO POULEN ESKIMONESS

MARCH 14TH

FROM ESKE BRUN

Your main task till further notice obtain fullest most reliable information and if possible without prejudice to main task also to eliminate enemy forces by capture or shooting. You are authorised use any means to this end and your weapons should be used rather than run least risk of being captured yourselves, or at the least sign among prisoners of resistance or attempts to escape. Immediately you have in your own judgment assembled enough men at the station, you may make journey proposed with necessary companions. Keep radio watch for possible detection enemy radio in neighbourhood. Be prepared for air attack. How many men will be at station when Olsen returns. Inform me for sake of identification from air how many men leave with how many sledges immediately on departure. Signal conditions of fjord ice with regard to possible plane landing. Signal winter ice and pack-ice conditions. Energy and judgment of great importance our future position in east Greenland. Remember enemy probably resolute so take no chances but shoot first. Brun.

Poulsen read this signal through and through, with the complicated feelings of most civilised people when war is declared on their behalf.

The signal told him exactly what to do, and made no attempt to tell him how to do it; and it gave him the governor's unqualified support. So far, it was all that any commander could have wanted. He had no logical doubt that it was right to eliminate the enemy; he only felt a half-conscious sadness that even the arctic peace had to be broken, and even the arctic sanity brought into line with the madness of the world outside. In Denmark, he would have welcomed an invitation like that to go out and fight a German on more or less equal terms. In the arctic, he still knew it was his duty, but he could not have pretended it was welcome. Of course, the men in Sabine Island were Germans, but it was hard to connect them with what the Germans were doing then in Europe. It was more natural to think of them as arctic people like himself, who could be asked in for a drink or a cup of coffee and a gossip; and he had to make a conscious effort to persuade himself that the very idea was absurd.

But still, he put these nebulous doubts behind him. The signal told him just what he wanted to know, and he was grateful. Some of the men were out when he finished deciphering it, and to make sure that they all saw it he stuck it up on the wall inside the door: an action with consequences which nobody could have foreseen.

The signal not only promised the personal support of Eske Brun, but it also made Poulsen expect the Americans very soon. The only Americans he had met in Greenland were the men on the coast guard ship which had supplied him in the summer, and one of the officers on board had told him he could count on American Air Force help whenever he needed it: planes could be there, he had said, at a few hours' notice any time, winter or summer. Now, Eske Brun's signal seemed to confirm it, and the men at Eskimoness began not only to watch the ice, expecting Germans, but also to watch the sky, expecting a fleet of American aircraft which would land on the ice or at least drop parachutists.

But in fact, this was quite impossible. Perhaps Poulsen had misunderstood what the officer said, or perhaps the officer had been talking out of turn. The truth was that Eskimoness was 750 miles from the nearest Air Force base, which was in Iceland: nearly as far as from London to Rome or from New York to Florida. There were not very many aircraft then which could do a round trip of 1500 miles carrying bombs or even parachutists. It was not very likely that at any particular moment the right kind of long-distance aircraft would happen to be in Iceland, and less likely still that they would have nothing better to do than to go to the help of half a dozen men. In any case, the only direct help they could have given might have been to drop a few machine-guns. There were no parachutists nearer than America or Europe, and nobody would have taken the chance of landing a heavy bomber on the ice. So Poulsen was really hundreds of miles beyond the range of help. But he did not know it, and he answered the governor's questions.

FROM ESKIMONESS
MARCH 15TH
TO BRUN GODTHAAB VIA SCORESBYSOUND

In front of station flat ice with hard packed snow surface and small snowdrifts greatest height 10 centimetres. Opposite Cape Otker ideal flat snowfree fjord ice with sand frozen into surface . . . Am sure plane could land most places. Recommend supply automatic weapons. Further on Olsen's arrival. POULSEN.

Everything Poulsen did in the next few weeks was done in the belief, which only dwindled slowly, that the American Air Force must be on the way.

In the meantime, Eske Brun had begun to worry about the order he had sent. It was all very well, he reflected, for him to have told the sledge patrol to shoot first, and he did not regret it. But if they carried out his order and got captured in spite of it, the Germans would be quite within their rights if they executed the whole patrol as *francs-tireurs*. The rules of war are archaic, illogical and ridiculous, but not even a colonial governor can change them; and what he had done, in legal terms, was to incite civilians to murder.

When he thought it over, he hit on an answer which pleased him enormously. There was nothing, so far as he knew, in international law to say that you had to be a king or a president to found an army, and so he decided to found one: the Greenland Army. He wrote out a set of commissions and appointments, and then sent a signal to Poulsen to tell him what he had done. Poulsen was made a captain, and the senior Dane at Scoresby Sound a lieutenant. Kurt Olsen, as second-in-command at Eskimoness, became a sergeant. On consideration, Eske Brun decided not to have any private soldiers in his army, and so he made all the rest of the Europeans corporals: Marius Jensen, Eli Knudsen, Peter Nielsen, and even Corporal Henry Rudi. It was impossible to provide them with uniforms before the summer, and anyhow it remained to design a uniform which could be worn in 90° of frost. He could not even send them their written and sealed appointments; but in the meantime, he told them to make armbands for themselves in blue and white, with a number of stars according to their rank. At its greatest strength, the Greenland Army mustered two officers, one sergeant and six corporals, together with six non-combatant Eskimo sledge drivers.

The whole arrangement had a charming element of farce in it, but it also had a perfectly serious intention and was practical and sensible. It might not have held water in an international court, but that was not the point. The point was that the Germans in Sabine Island could hardly know that the Greenland Army was on the small side and a comparatively recent institution. If the worst came to the worst, its members could claim to be treated as prisoners of war, and by the time international jurists got to work on it, nobody would care what they decided.

After the crisis and the anxiety were over, and the governor could allow himself to see the funny side of what he had done, he began to enjoy calling himself the General. At the time, he would have given anything to be in northeast Greenland with his troops, but of course it was physically impossible for him to get there; and in later years he was heard to say ruefully that like all good generals he had stayed five hundred miles behind the firing line.

Anyhow, the founding of the new army gave Poulsen an official rank at last, and it gave all the men at Eskimoness something to laugh about. When they had all got over their surprise, and sewn their arm-bands, and got tired of saluting Poulsen and pulling Henry Rudi's leg for having achieved two stripes so late in life, they went back to work on their fortifications with extra confidence. The Greenland Army: it did not want to fight, but if it had to, every man in it had a rifle and could hit a musk-ox at a thousand yards.

14

RITTER HAD also sent a signal back to his headquarters, as soon as Dr. Weiss had come in with the news that the three sledge drivers had disappeared. He had to assume that they had got back to Eskimoness alive, and so he had to report that his base had been discovered. He also asked for orders, but the answer he got was not nearly so satisfactory as Poulsen's. It simply told him to use his own discretion; and in all the circumstances that was just what Ritter did not want to do. He would much rather have had a definite order, which might have helped him to silence his own conscience and prevented any criticism from the Nazis.

Poulsen and Marius had been surprised that the Germans did not attack Eskimoness the very day that Marius returned. The reason was so simple that they had not thought of it. The Germans had captured three excellent dog teams, but they did not know how to drive them, and they had no other kind of transport. Ritter himself had driven dogs a little in Spitzbergen, and even Weiss and his companions, on the morning after the encounter at Cape Wynn, had found to their own surprise that the dogs which seemed so fearsome in the darkness were quite friendly in the daylight, and they had managed to harness them and drive the teams away. But the ten-mile journey back to Hansa Bay had been a series of comic accidents, with the dogs bewildered by foreign shouts and all pulling in opposite directions. Ritter would have liked to go to Eskimoness at once, but until his men had learned to manage dogs, it was impossible for him to get there.

The Germans set to work at sledging with enthusiasm. It was a new kind of sport for them, and a change from the tedious routine of Hansa Bay. Ritter taught them what he knew about it, and also put in some practice on his own; and between his sledge practices, he began to read through Marius Jensen's log book. In his travels, he had learned a good many languages: one of them was English, and another was Norwegian, which he had picked up in Spitzbergen. Anyone who can speak Norwegian can also read Danish, which is very much like it, and his only difficulty was in decyphering Marius's writing. When he had read it all, there was not very much more for him to learn about the sledge patrol. He knew its strength and guessed it was only armed with rifles, and he knew more or less where all its members had been when Marius had started on his journey.

From a strictly military point of view, when Eske Brun had told the patrol to keep logs of their journeys, and when Marius had left his lying on the table, they had presented Ritter with the kind of advantage that generals dream about. But from a psychological point of view, the captured log book did him more harm than good. It told him far too much about his opponents. They were exactly the kind of people he had known in Spitzbergen and come to like so much. They were living exactly the sort of life he had enjoyed. He found himself almost wishing he was with them, driving freely about the coast instead of sitting imprisoned with his Nazis. What upset him most of all was to read the name of Henry Rudi. He had once met Rudi in Spitzbergen, and had often heard stories about him, as the doyen of arctic hunters, and also as a man with a sense of humour who was good company on a winter night.

By military standards, perhaps it is always bad for a soldier to know too much about his enemy, in case he is reminded too clearly that his enemy is as human as himself. It is best for a whole-hearted soldier to persuade himself, or be persuaded, that his enemies as individuals have all the worst qualities of their nation, even though the most elementary common sense says that some of them are people he would like or even admire if he met them; otherwise wars could never be begun. Perhaps this delusion had begun to wear thin in other countries by 1943. Certainly it seemed nonsense in Greenland. The men in the sledge patrol suspected that the men in Hansa Bay, even though they were Germans, were also reasonable people: Ritter, on the other side, knew with certainty that the sledge patrol men were the sort of men he could have felt at home with, if the far-away authorities of Berlin had not decreed that they were enemies.

Nevertheless, he had to look at the situation from a military point of view. He had no wish to do the Danes any harm, but at least he had to do the best he could to protect his base and the men under his command. Now that the base had been detected, he took it for granted that sooner or later it would be bombed; but he knew more than Poulsen about aircraft, and did not make the mistake of thinking the Americans would have an easy job. He had done all he could to make it difficult by camouflaging his installations and tucking them away among the hills. When he thought it out, there were only two other things that he could do. One was to move the base and hide it somewhere else. The other was to make sure that the Americans, when they came, would not have any weather reports to guide them. He did not know for certain if weather reports were already being sent out from Eskimoness; but so long as there was a radio station there, it was certain the Americans would use it when the time came, to give them reports of local visibility and wind and cloud conditions.

So it was clearly his military duty to smash up the radio transmitter at Eskimoness; and his conscience had nothing to say against it. Of course, he could not expect the Danes to agree, but he hoped to persuade them it was not worth shedding blood about it; and as he was the only one of the Germans who could make himself understood in Danish, he would have to lead the expedition himself. Moving the base was a bigger job, and might come later. But both of these jobs depended on mastering the dog teams.

By the end of a week, the dogs had settled down, and his men were quite confident.

15

BY THE end of the week, the Danes at Eskimoness were beginning to feel secure. Nothing had happened, the defence works were complete, and the first feeling of alarm was wearing off. They were puzzled that neither the Germans nor the Americans had come; but it had started to look as if neither were ever coming.

The Eskimos, on the other hand, got more and more alarmed. The situation was more frightening for them than it was for the Danes; for whereas the Danes understood more or less what the war was about, the whole conception of war was a mystery to the Eskimos, and so they suffered all the terrors of unknown imaginary dangers. Nothing in their upbringing had prepared them for fighting. They only had the vaguest idea of European geography, and none at all of politics or ideologies. On the other hand, they knew their Bible well. No doubt they had read of Old Testament wars, but that was not much help to them; and the Christianity which was the whole basis of life at

Scoresby Sound was simple. It had not made the effort which European Christianity had made to adjust itself to modern wars. It merely said to its people: Thou shalt not kill.

Poulsen knew he could not expect them to take any part in defending the station, and anyhow he had been told not to get them mixed up in fighting; and so he sent Aparte and Mikael away with their sledges to Ella Island, to tell any of the men who happened to be there to come north as reinforcements.

Kurt Olsen had come back from his trip to Hold With Hope, and so there was only one man in the northern section of the patrol who had not yet been warned what was happening; and that was Peter Nielsen. He was still somewhere in the far north round Hochstetter Foreland, and he was till expecting Marius Jensen, who had been on his way there to join him when all the trouble started. Marius and Poulsen were both worried about Peter. They thought that sooner or later he himself would get worried about Marius, and then he might come south and run into Sabine Island alone from the opposite direction. The only way to stop him was to go up north to try to find him. Poulsen would have liked to send the other two Eskimos, so that he could keep all his corporals at home; but the route to the north led through Sandodden and the Kuppel Pass, within twenty miles of Sabine Island, and he knew without bothering to ask them that he would never be able to persuade them to go.

However, he also knew that he would never forgive himself if he let Peter get captured without even trying to warn him; and besides, it seemed unenterprising to sit cowering any longer and waiting for the Germans to take the initiative. So he made up his mind to let Marius and Eli Knudsen go to look for Peter, and to go himself on a reconnaissance farther east. As they were short of dogs, the teams had to be divided to give Marius enough to travel with.

Poulsen gave strict orders to the others. They were to go north by the usual route by Sandodden and the Kuppel Pass, and they were never to approach a hut without driving right round it first to make sure that no tracks led into it. They were to come back by a different pass farther inland across Wollaston Foreland, and round the west side of Clavering Island. It was a longer route and a more difficult pass to cross, but it was farther from Sabine Island. They agreed; but he knew from experience of the hunters that once they were out on their own they would interpret his orders pretty freely.

His own plan was to take the Eskimo Evald, and Evald's sledge, and escort the others as far as Sandodden, and then go on as far as he could to the eastward, to make a first reconnaissance. As soon as he got a chance, he meant to go and have a look at Hansa Bay itself. That could not be done by sledge, because a sledge would have to keep to the ice and would be certain to be seen; but he reckoned that if he went alone on skis across the hills, he might be able to reach the rim of the mountains round Hansa Bay and look down into the bay to see what was hidden there. However, that was an ambitious plan which would take at least a week; and it would have to wait until all the others were assembled at Eskimoness to defend it while he was away.

In the meantime, he and Evald, with Marius and Knudsen, went together as far as Sandodden and spend the night there. So far, they were on the route which the Germans would have to use if they were coming to Eskimoness; but even so, Poulsen was uneasy at leaving so few men behind there. There were only three of them: Kurt Olsen, Henry Rudi and William the Eskimo. As Kurt Olsen had to do the weather broadcasts, and the others had all the work of running the station, they would not even be able to keep an effective watch; and as for defending the place, it might almost as well have been empty. But with a force of seven men, he had to take some chances.

After the night at Sandodden, Marius and Knudsen set off for the Kuppel Pass, and Poulsen and Evald turned back and started to fol-low the shore to the eastward: exactly the same route that Marius had taken on his unlucky journey, and exactly the route that the Germans would probably take if they ever came in to attack.

From the beginning, there was an eerie feel about the coast beyond Sandodden. As far as that, the ground was familiar, but beyond it the patrol had seldom ventured, and now it felt like enemy territory. Evald was very nervous. The sea-ice was so rough that sledges or Germans might easily have been hidden among its ridges, and the black cliffs which brooded silently above it on the left seemed menacing. For Evald, to whom the German threat was almost supernatural, it was easy to imagine eyes watching from the rocks above, and figures lurking behind the endless mounds of ice. To try to calm him, Poulsen climbed up the snow-covered scree at the cliff foot, so that he had a more distant view along the ice. He started to walk along up there, a hundred feet or so above the ice, and told Evald to follow him with the sledge, down on the ice and a little way behind. In that way, he could have given Evald plenty of warning if anyone was coming; but it was slow work to plough a track along the soft unstable slope, and by nightfall they had only covered a dozen miles.

They pitched a tent that night in a gully at the foot of the cliffs. The darkness only added to Evald's fears; and in fact they were in such a vulnerable position that there was nothing much that Poulsen could say to reassure him. If the Germans were on their way to Eskimoness, they might have decided to move in the night and lie up in the daytime, and they would have to pass close to the tent and would see the tracks and alarm the dogs. Evald burst into tears, and told Poulsen about his father and mother and said he was too young to die. Poulsen advised him to put his trust in God, and reminded him of Christ's saying about the sparrows. That seemed to comfort him, but he was much too upset to lie down and sleep, and the whole of the night passed in prayers and religious discussion in the Eskimo language. Poulsen saw it was hopeless to try to take Evald farther. By day, their progress would be slow, and by night he would not sleep;

and the farther they went, the worse it was going to be. Besides, he was sorry for him. It was a deadlock: he could not go on alone without a sledge, and it seemed unfair to leave Evald to find his own way home on foot. There was nothing for it but to go back together.

In the morning after his sleepless night, before they turned back to the west, Poulsen climbed as high as he could up the cliffs with his glasses and looked towards the east. He could see the island, thirty miles away, and he could have seen a dog team more than half as far as that if there had been one; but there was absolutely nothing on the ice.

Anyhow, Rudi and Olsen were glad to see him back at the station, where three effective rifles were at least a bit better than two. He arrived there on the 21st of March: ten days after Marius's first encounter. Eskimoness was sinking back into something like its old routine. The only visible difference was the fortifications which cluttered up the sitting-room window, and the only difference in the daily life was that the Eskimos went out on short patrols by day, to keep an eye on the immediate approaches, and that by night the three Europeans took turns on watch outside.

After Evald's behaviour on the journey, it was obvious that the only thing to do with him and William, if there ever was an attack, was to get them out of the way as quickly as possible. It was no good being annoyed with them for what looked like cowardice. Faced with a bear, they would have been as brave as anyone; and many people's courage fails when they are faced with something they cannot understand. Poulsen knew he had never succeeded in explaining to them, in the cumbrous Eskimo language, any convincing reason why they should shoot at Germans. So he gave them the simplest possible orders. They were to keep one of the two remaining dog teams well out of sight of the house. If anything happened, they were to harness the team at once and drive to a point on the shore to the westward and wait. If they thought it was too dangerous to wait there, they could drive to a hut twelve miles away on the other side of the bay. If even that looked dangerous, they could go to Ella Island. They said they understood.

The three Europeans also had their action stations. Poulsen's was in front of the house, Rudi's in a sand-bagged post to the west of it, and Kurt Olsen's about fifty yards away to the east on top of a little rise. With all this settled, they relaxed as well as they could to wait for Marius, Eli Knudsen, and Peter Nielsen. They might get back in a week; and when they came in and doubled the effective strength, things would be very different. It would be time enough then to think of carrying the war to the enemy's camp.

On the evening of March 23rd, before it was dark, Poulsen went the rounds of his station alone, far enough out on the ice to see along the coast, and round to the back of the small peninsula on which the house was built. He stopped to talk to the dogs, having a word with each one in turn so that none of them should be jealous. They jumped up and licked him and whined with pleasure and he scratched them behind their ears, and his thoughts were not particularly military. Among other things, he was thinking about a barrel of beer. Danish Government outposts were always well stocked with wines and spirits, on the theory that a man who could be trusted to winter there at all could also be trusted not to drink himself to death; but beer was never sent up there because it took up too much space in the supply ships. Instead, the stations were supplied with the ingredients for making it, and Poulsen was in the middle of the process. He had an oil drum full of it in the house, and he meant to go through the final stage of brewing before he went to bed.

He finished it at eleven o'clock that night, just about the time when Kurt Olsen was starting the weather broadcast in the radio room next door. He was standing there in his shirt sleeves, looking at his barrel with a feeling of satisfaction, when Henry Rudi put his head in at the door.

"Poulsen," he shouted, "Poulsen! I think there's somebody on the ice."

Poulsen snatched up his rifle. "Kurt," he called. "Outside!"

"I'm just starting the report," Kurt Olsen answered.

"Get to your post!" Poulsen shouted over his shoulder. He ran to the door.

Outside, it was pitch dark, for the sky was overcast. He could just see the outline of his motor boat which was drawn up on the beach sixty yards away. Everything was as silent as ever. Rudi had gone. He stood alone and listened. The dogs were stirring. And then, out on the ice beyond the shore, he heard a stealthy movement.

"Who's there?" he shouted.

The movement stopped, and nobody answered. The dogs began to howl. Could a bear have mad a noise like that, he wondered; or could it be Marius in trouble? Then from the darkness a voice in broken Danish shouted, "Who are you?"

That answer told Poulsen everything. "What do you want here?" he asked in German, and there was another silence.

"I want to speak to Herr Poulsen," the bodiless voice replied.

Poulsen was astonished and shaken to hear his own name. A defensive instinct told him not to give himself away. "You can't talk to him to-night," he shouted. "You can come back in the daylight." He stood there tense with his finger on the trigger, trying to catch a glimpse of his opponent, but the voice came to him disembodied from the vague greyness of the ice.

"Can I speak to Herr Olsen or Herr Rudi?" it asked.

Poulsen's thoughts were racing ahead of his words. The Germans knew exactly who was at the station: then they must have broken the ciphers: they must know how few men there were and how weakly they were armed. He heard movements again and shouted, "Get back from the beach."

"I must speak to Herr Poulsen, or else Herr Rudi or Herr Olsen," the voice insisted.

"What about?" Poulsen asked. "How many of you?"

The voice replied with something that sounded like a name.

"One man can come across the beach," Poulsen said. "Unarmed."

The voice said: "Do you intend to offer armed resistance?"

"Yes," Poulsen shouted; and at that word machine-gun fire burst out and tracer bullets flew at him from the ice. He dropped to one knee and raised his rifle and fired towards the muzzle-flashes a hundred yards away, but it was so dark he could not see the sights of his rifle, and the flashes from his own gun seemed to draw the fire down on him. He jumped into cover behind a packing-case full of ice and as he went down bullets smacked into it and threw chips of ice and frozen earth into his face.

He had never in his life seen tracer bullets, but he knew what they were. The streaks of greenish light sailed towards him from two or three directions, and he knew from the very first moment that they were a weapon he could not fight against: for a machine-gun with tracers can be aimed like a hose, but a rifle in the dark when one cannot see the sights is perfectly useless and cannot be aimed at all. He ran round the house to try to find the others and met Henry Rudi standing there as if he were paralysed. Another burst of fire came overhead, and he pushed Rudi down and went on to look for Olsen. A concentration of bullets was pouring over Olsen's post, as if he had been firing and had shown where he was. Poulsen shouted to him but there was no answer. He turned back towards the house and got a clear sight of the flash of a machine-gun again, and he shot at it. Again it seemed that when he fired, the machine-gun was turned on him.

Rudi had disappeared. The hammering of the machine-guns and the criss-cross of bullets soaring over the flat ground beside the house confused Poulsen so that he could not tell which side the Germans were coming from, and he thought he was surrounded. He went back for Olsen, but his post was still under fire, and Olsen did not answer when he shouted. He could not find anyone or do anything more, and if he stayed where he was for another few seconds he was going to be killed or captured; so he ran across the level behind the house, still under fire, and went a little way up the hill beyond it.

Then he stopped to look back. Most of the firing died away, and only one gun went on in occasional bursts from the eastward. He began to be conscious of something else: the cold. And slowly, as his nerves calmed a little, he began to realise more fully what had happened. In less than ten minutes, the house had been lost, and everything that was in it. His men were dead or scattered. He was still only wearing a shirt and trousers and a pair of sealskin boots which he had used as bedroom slippers. There were approximately 45° of frost, and the nearest help was at Ella Island, two hundred miles away.

16

RITTER WAS sick at heart. He had not been able to understand exactly what the man in front of the house had been saying, either because of the distance and the noise the dogs were making, or because they were both speaking a mixture of Danish and German. He had had to get into the house, either by persuasion or else by force, because otherwise he would have been caught on the open ice in daylight.

The only thing he had heard perfectly clearly was the other man's answer when he had asked if he meant to resist. The man had used the German *jawohl,* and there had been no doubt about it. It had dashed Ritter's hopes of more or less peaceful persuasion, and he had squeezed the trigger at once. That was his second plan: to shoot over their heads, to show the Danes what they were up against, and frighten them into surrender.

But that had gone wrong. It had been much too thorough, and had put an end to any idea of talk, because no man in his senses would have talked to him willingly after what he and his men had done. For one thing, he had not allowed for such absolute darkness. He had been dazzled by the muzzle flashes of his own gun and had hardly been able to tell where his shots were going, in spite of the tracer; and when the five men he had brought with him had taken up the shooting, he had seen they were firing low and hitting the house and sweeping the ground outside it. Whether they meant to or not, they were shooting to kill. He could not tell them to stop, they were too widely scattered and there was too much noise. Even while his finger was on the trigger, his conscience and his military self were still at war. It was exactly what he had been afraid would happen: he was faced with a military duty which his conscience said was wrong: and because he had put off making up his mind, and gone on too long in a futile hope that he could put if off for ever, he had robbed himself of any chance to make a free decision when the moment came. Now, through his orders, or through his lack of clear precise orders, he believed that one man at least was being killed. In the seven minutes that the shooting lasted, Ritter had accused himself of murder, and found nothing to be said in his defence.

Before the firing stopped Ritter began to advance, with Nowotny, the Czech engineer, close behind him, over the shore-ice and up the gentle slope towards the house, carrying his hot machine-gun in his had. He had not bothered to reload it. He did not care in the least by then what happened to him. Let the Danes shoot if they were still alive: he wanted them to be alive, not dead. He wanted, for a brief moment, to die, but to die without a murder on his hands; life was too much for him, and death, he thought, as many men have thought before and since, was a welcome escape, the only possible escape from all his problems. As he walked up the sixty yards of shore he was thinking, with a despairing cynicism unusual in him, that a death which could be called a hero's death would be convenient, because it would silence his accusers and make sure of the safety of his wife and his daughter. For himself, he only cared about one thing at that moment: that he would not find a dead man lying by the door.

Such problems are seldom solved so easily. There was no corpse by the door: nobody shot at him: nobody answered his shout. He walked straight to the door and threw it open. It was dark inside. He flashed his torch round the room, found the electric light switch and turned it on; and while his eyes were still dazzled he stood there, an easy target. Almost the first thing he saw was the signal from Eske Brun, still hanging where Poulsen had pinned it to the wall: and as his men came rushing in behind him with guns at the ready and started to search the house, he read it through: "Eliminate enemy forces by capture or shooting—take no chances but shoot first." There was no compromise there, no possible hint of a peaceful solution. It reminded him almost brutally that whatever he might want himself, he had put himself outside the pale of the arctic community, simply because he had become a German officer and Nazi Germany had set the world at bay.

It only took a very short time for his men to make sure there was nobody left in the house or the outbuildings. He took the usual precautions against a counter-attack, and then thoughtfully set to work to give Eskimoness a thorough inspection.

Having captured the post, he had to decide what to do with it. All he had meant to do was to smash up the radio and perhaps get the Danes to accept some kind of parole not to hale the Americans against him. But the Governor's signal had put things in a different light. It suggested that Eskimoness might not only be used as an advanced radio station to help the American Air Force, but also perhaps as a base for an attack against him over the ice, if the Danes had any more forces they could rally. If he had been able to talk to the Danes, he could have found out, he supposed, whether this was a serious risk or not; but as they had gone, he could only play for safety and put the whole place out of action once and for all. He did not want to do it. It offended his sense of arctic propriety. He had been spared the remorse he would have felt if one of the Danes had been shot, but he knew that to wreck a man's house in the arctic might condemn him to a death which was only a little slower. He knew there was a possibility that Henry Rudi and Poulsen, or whoever it was who had been there, might get away to some other place of safety; but in his experience it was only a slender chance, a mere question of whether a blizzard happened to catch them on the way.

Yet although he did not want to do it, he was afraid not to do it. Schmidt was with him and he did not dare to let it be said that he had captured the enemy's base and then left it intact for the enemy to use. The military risk of doing so might really be very small, but it would look like an act of lunacy in a military report.

In the end, Ritter once more discovered a compromise. First, he decided to wait, to give the Danes a fair chance to come back if they were still in hiding in the hills. After Marius Jensen's disappearance, he hardly expected them; but on the other hand, they were much farther from any help than Marius Jensen had been, and he supposed that if they were still somewhere close at hand, and were hungry or in danger of freezing, they might be inclined to give in.

The second part of his compromise was to decide to leave one small outhouse standing. To some extent, that salved his arctic conscience. If any traveller happened to come along when he had gone, depending on Eskimoness for rest or shelter in a storm, the smallest of the huts would be enough to save his life; but on the other hand it would be no use at all to a military force of the size the Danes would need for a counter-attack on Hansa Bay.

So Ritter and his men stayed there for two days. They were surprised to find what a comfortable home the Danes had been able to make. The American food was much better than their own, and the quarters were much more spacious and better furnished. Ritter himself was embarrassed to find the ample stock of drinks. The Sachsen had brought a certain amount of spirits with her, but early in the winter he had had so much trouble with a few drunks in his crew that he had poured the remains of it overboard, which had very much annoyed the men in question. Now, after several months without a drink at all, his men were confronted with limitless drink for the taking, and he did not trust them; so he broke all the Danish bottles, and he and the other Germans had to content themselves with Poulsen's drum of beer.

Ritter inspected every item of equipment in the house, and glanced through all the papers he could find. There was a mass of old letters addressed to Henry Rudi, Poulsen's passport and radio certificate, family photographs, a certain amount of money and all the sentimental odds and ends which men accumulate. There was also another log book, Kurt Olsen's, which told Ritter of Poulsen's plan to spy on the German base from the Sabine hills; and here and there, there was a very large collection of valuable furs. Ritter took the log book, but he collected all the personal possessions of the Danes, including the furs, and put them in the little hut which had been used for curing skins. As a symbol, he also hauled down the Danish flag and folded it up and put it with the furs; and then he wrote a message and nailed it up inside the little hut:

The U.S.A. protects its defence interests here in Greenland. We do the same. We are not at war with Denmark. But your governor has given orders to capture or shoot us, and you are giving weather reports to the enemy. You are therefore making Greenland a theatre of war. We have stayed quietly at our post without attacking you. But if you want war you shall have war. Remember that if you use illegal weapons (dum-dum bullets) such as we have found here, you must take the consequences, because you will put yourselves outside the rules of war. Note that we have put all personal property of your hunters and all

furs in this hut, while we have destroyed the radio apparatus
operating for the U.S.A.

signed: H. Ritter,
Commander of the Wehrmacht Unit, Eskimoness

But it was nearly six months before this note was found, and it never
came into the hands of the sledge patrol.*

After they had finished these preparations, Ritter and his party
smashed the radio, shot some of the dogs because they could not
take all of them away, and poured petrol in the wooden house and
set it on fire. It blazed furiously, and soon there was nothing of Eskimoness left except its ashes, glowing in a pit which the heat had
melted in the snow.

---

* Kurt Olsen's log book, which Ritter took with him to Hansa Bay, was found after the war in
the building which had been the Gestapo's offices in Copenhagen. Nobody knows exactly
how it got there.

17

IF RITTER had known exactly what had happened to Poulsen, he would have had a good reason for feeling remorseful, because nobody, on that night of March 23rd, could have said that Poulsen had any reasonable chance at all of saving his own life, except by going back to the house and trusting himself to the mercy of the Germans.

Forty-five degrees of frost is not cold for a Greenland night in March; but it is cold enough to be dangerous. It is as far below freezing point as a warm summer day in Europe is above it. If it had only just been freezing, a man dressed as Poulsen was dressed would not have suffered anything worse than discomfort: the internal warmth of his body, circulated by his blood, would have kept his flesh from freezing. But at forty-five degrees of frost, the physiological effects of cold are naturally much more violent. The warmth of the blood is not enough to replace the loss of heat in parts of the body which are exposed, and the fluids in them freeze and stop the circulation. This is frostbite. Within a short time, if the frozen flesh is not thawed out again, it dies.

The only way to avoid frostbite is to wear proper clothes and to be alert for the first signs of its attacks. At first, it only leads to numbness, not to pain; the pain comes when the flesh is thawed again. So it may not be noticed before a lot of damage has been done; and when it is very cold, travellers get into the habit of screwing up their faces, or feeling their faces with their fingers from time to time, to find out whether the skin is getting stiff. Two men together keep an eye on each other's faces, to look for white patches on them. The fingers and feet are also often attacked. If frostbite starts, the traveller immediately stops whatever he is doing to warm the affected part. He borrows warmth from his companion if he has one. If it is bad, he pitches his tent at once. It is a horrible affliction. Everyone in the arctic winter takes it very seriously. The more experienced the traveller, the more careful he is about it.

Poulsen, standing on the hillside above Eskimoness that night, in his shirt and trousers and his skin shoes with no socks inside them, had no protection at all against frostbite and he knew it. But he did not go back to the house. By then, he was so angry with the Germans that he would probably have faced the quickest most violent death in preference to begging them for mercy; and he was so angry with himself, for what he regarded as his own failure, that he would have gone through any ordeal which might have helped to retrieve the situation. So, in his absurdly inadequate clothes, he turned away from his captured home and began to walk, although he knew that nobody in the history of the arctic had done such a foolish thing before, and that in all foreseeable probability he was starting a journey which would end in his death or make him a scarred and helpless cripple.

From the beginning, he was clear enough in his head to make reasonable plans. First, he went to a place where he knew Henry Rudi had hidden a rucksack, and he was thankful to find it gone. So the old man had at least got away from the house. He was less hopeful about Kurt Olsen, and was afraid he had been killed, or wounded and captured. He took it for granted that the two Eskimos had gone with their dog sledge. There had been plenty of time for them to get to the place where the dogs had been hidden before the shooting started, and it was well out of range. By the time he escaped himself, they should have been miles away.

Nest he ran to the cache he had laid in the hills. He was encouraged to find somebody had been there before him and taken some of the food. It might only have been Rudi, but he hoped it was Olsen, too. The cache contained tents and sleeping-bags and food; but when he had laid it, he had never thought of anyone leaving the house in such a hurry that he would have to go without his clothes, and so he had not left any there. He was very cold already. A tent was no use to him, because he had no sledge and the tents were too heavy to carry; so he cut one up into pieces with his knife. He wrapped a large piece round him like a cloak, with a flap of it over his head, and he tied it in place with some bits of guy ropes; and he took two smaller pieces and wrapped his hands in them, tying them round his wrists with difficulty because his hands were already getting numb. He took a sleeping-bag and put some food in it, and rolled it up and hoisted it on his back. Equipped in this incongruous style, he first went back towards the house to have a last search for Olsen. But there was nothing to be seen except one man who seemed to be on watch outside the door; and before daylight he began to stumble towards the west.

His first objective was Henry Rudi's hut at Revet. Revet was no use as a permanent refuge. There were no stores or equipment there. Ella Island, two hundred miles away, was the only place where he could equip himself again and make a fresh start in the fight; but he had not had time to think of any possible way of getting to Ella Island, and had not yet admitted to himself that he might simply have to walk there. Anyhow, there were several reasons for going to Revet first. For one thing, a portable radio transmitter had been left there in the autumn, and if it was still in working order, he might be able to send a signal to Scoresby Sound. Secondly, the three men who had been up north had been told to come back that way. If he was very lucky, he might meet them and their sledges; but in any case he knew they would go into the hut when they passed it, and he had to leave them a warning not to go on to Eskimoness. Thirdly, Revet had been inhabited for many years, and he hoped he would find some cast-off clothes there.

It was thirty-five miles to Revet. Of course, he could have walked that far without stopping, and that might have been the best thing to do, to keep the cold out; but along the shore of Clavering Island, he would have been visible for a long way in the daylight, and he expected the Germans to make a sortie with their sledges to round up prisoners. So in the early dawn he stopped at a hunting hut and had some food, and then, in case they found the hut, he climbed a little way up the mountains at the back of it, and found a sheltered gully, and spread his sleeping-bag on the snow and got wearily into it, to sleep the daylight through.

Once Poulsen got over the anger which naturally results from being shot at, he became very despondent. He lay shivering that night in his sleeping-bag alone on the frozen hill, seeing himself as an utter failure. He had lost his base, and lost touch with all his men. His dogs were gone, and he was a helpless fugitive. The Germans were free, with his dogs, to range the coast and destroy the hunting stations and perhaps even attack the peaceful settlement at Scoresby Sound itself. Worst of all was his recollection of that sentence in the signal from Eske Brun: "Energy and judgment of great importance our future position in East Greenland." He knew why Eske Brun had put it in. It was to remind him that he was not just the commander of a dozen men, but was being held responsible for looking after the whole of that enormous area of the colony. Perhaps, he thought, because he had failed, Norwegians or Americans or British would have to step in to take over the patrol from the Danes, and then perhaps Denmark would lose the north-east coast for ever. That was his bitterest thought.

Strangely enough, he did not think of putting the blame on anyone but himself. If he had had a little experience as a soldier, it might have occurred to him that to be told to "eliminate" an enemy, in the course of a modern war, when one had nothing but a hunting rifle to do it with, was to say the least an optimistic order. But he himself had not expected machine-guns and tracer bullets, simply because nobody had ever used such things in Greenland; and he never thought of blaming Eske Brun for not foreseeing what they were up against. The only resentment he felt at all was against the Americans, for not coming at once to help him; and of course that resentment was misplaced, as he learned much later on, because they could not help him, and if he thought they had promised help it was all a misunderstanding. For Poulsen, the 24th of March passed by in misery: physical misery from the cold, which even penetrated the sleeping-bag, and mental misery at the picture of his failure. He dozed a little; and at dusk he got up and walked on along the shore to Revet.

The second night's walk can only have been agony, though in the way of people who are bitterly disappointed in themselves, he almost welcomed pain and afterwards made light of it. Sharp edges of ice, and rocks along the shore, cut the soles of his feet through the soft thin skin of his shoes. The first stages of frostbite showed themselves in his hands and face and ears and feet. His blood temperature must have fallen very low, because he had a feeling of unnatural lassitude and could hardly keep himself awake. He could not have walked very far that night, in those conditions, before he fell down and died. Luckily, it was only twenty-three miles more to Revet from the place where he had slept; and he had been perfectly fit before he got frozen and would normally have walked that distance without thinking twice about it. But that night, when at last he reached the hut, and warmth and a temporary safety seemed to be in his grasp, he was so exhausted and his hands were so bad that he could not move his fingers to turn the door knob. For some minutes, while he struggled to open the door, he had to face the irony of dying there on the very doorstep, because if he could not get in, he was much too far gone to reach any other hut. He went down on his knees in the end, and got hold of the knob between his wrists; and at long last he turned it, and crawled inside.

The stove was warm. Somebody had been there, and only gone that night. In the dark, Poulsen held his frozen hands against the stove and felt the searing pain come into them as they thawed. As soon as he could move them, he fumbled round for matches, and lit the fire which was laid, and the paraffin lamp; and then he saw a scribbled note which was lying on the table:

> *Don't go to Eskimoness. Germans have captured it. Think Poulsen was killed. We others all right.*
> *Olsen Rudi*

That took a weight off his mind. It even made him smile; and before he left the hut, he crossed out the words "Think Poulsen was killed," and wrote at the bottom: "Am O.K."

But in fact, he was only O.K. in the sense that he was not dead yet. He had patches of first-degree frostbite all over him; but in the first degree, before the tissues are damaged, frostbite heals itself after the extremely painful process of thawing is over. He was also very tired and his feet were very sore. But the worst of it was that he knew quite well that his difficulties had only just begun.

The words "we others" in Olsen and Rudi's note made him think that all four of the others were together, Olsen and Rudi and the two Eskimos; and if they were, they presumably had the Eskimos' sledge. As the stove had been warm when he came in, they were obviously not very far away. But all he wanted in the world just then was warmth and food and sleep, and he was simply unable to go out again to try to track them in the darkness. So he ate, and thawed himself, and tried the portable radio, but its batteries were flat. He scrounged round the hut and its loft, and as he had hoped, he found a few dirty old worn-out clothes, including an anorak and a pair of boots; and then, because he was still only half a day's sledge journey away from the Germans, and Revet was one of the most likely places for them to look for him, he took the sleeping-bag up into the hills and slept in the snow again: more soundly, now that he knew his friends had got away.

That evening, when he woke again, he felt a lot better, and he was able to look squarely at the fact that he had no option: he would have to try to walk to Ella just as he was, without any equipment at all. The others, he supposed, were a day ahead of him, and he was left behind. Even if they only had one sledge between the four of them, they would be able to travel faster than he could. Marius Jensen, Knudsen and Peter Nielsen must still be away to the northward, but there was no knowing how long it would be before they came south, and he could not afford to wait. The most urgent thing was to get to Ella and use the radio there to report what had happened to Eske Brun, and then to collect the scattered forces into a unit again.

Shortly before it was dark on March 25th, at the end of the second day after the attack, he went down again to Henry Rudi's hut to look for anything else which might be useful on the journey. The boots he had found were much too big for him, and he still had no socks. But there were plenty of old sacks which had been used for coal and flour, so he cut up sacks and made them into stockings as well as he could, tying the loose ends around his legs. He found an old pair of skis and took some matches. Rather than take any of the cooking utensils which belonged to the hut, he chose an empty meat tin so that he would be sure to have something to melt snow in in the huts on the way. He could have worn the skis, but they would not have helped him much on the hard fjord ice, and he would have had to carry the sleeping-bag and the tin and the remains of his food; so instead, he fastened the skis together, and wrapped the tin and the food in the sleeping bag and lashed it on the skis so that he could tow the whole lot behind him like a sledge. So he had nothing to carry, except of course his rifle.

The sledge patrol was used to travelling light, but even by the patrol's standard Poulsen's equipment made a meagre inventory: one pair of discarded skis, one sleeping-bag, one empty tin, a box of matches, a rifle and a knife, and food for about two days; and that was all.

When he was ready, he laid a fresh fire in the stove at Revet, in accordance with the custom, filled the paraffin lamp and left it ready on the table, and then went out and shut the door behind him. On the door he drew three circles, which is a private sign to the northern party which meant "I have gone south." He fastened a string to the front of the pair of skis and tied it round his waist, and then went down on to the ice and turned southward, with two hundred miles of mountain and fjord ahead of him.

18

POULSEN KNEW the way to Ella Island well, because he had travelled it several times by sledge. To begin with, it led across the bay called Godthaab's Gulf, which is 25 miles long and about the same in breadth, and the second stage was up the narrow fjord which is called Loch Fyne: another 25 miles to the head of it.

Through the whole of this first fifty miles, he expected to meet the Germans. He kept alert for tracks or the sound of dogs, although he did not know what he would do if he met them. There was not very much that he could do. He could not have hidden himself or escaped them, because their dogs would have scented him and run him down, and he had learned that it was not much use to fight against machine-guns with a rifle.

Through the same fifty miles, he also expected a blizzard. The weather had been settled for a long time, and it was too much to hope that it would stay fine much longer, so early in the year. Against a blizzard, he would have been as helpless as he was against the Germans, especially on the open ice of Godthaab's Gulf. There is an accepted way for a man without a tent to protect himself against a blizzard: he can dig himself a burrow in a snowdrift, and lie in it in his sleeping-bag. If he has a Primus stove, he can survive a long time underneath the snow. But Poulsen had no Primus, and nothing to dig with except his hands, and while he was crossing the ice it was a very long way to any snowdrift. If the weather had broken that night, there would not have been anything left for him to do except to die as gracefully as he could.

But the weather held, and the Germans were not to be seen. He walked on and on across the gulf throughout the night: a ski stick in one hand, the skis sliding silently behind him, the line gently tugging at his waist, his breath hanging in a cloud on the quiet air and turning to ice in the stubble of his beard and the rim of the hood of his borrowed anorak. All round him on the shores of the gulf he could see the dark loom of the mountains, deceptively close; between them, on the right, the gleam of the tongues of a great glacier which flows from the ice cap. An hour's hard going made only the slightest difference to this landscape, for the mountains hardly shifted, and the flat ice of the foreground was always exactly the same. At dawn, he was still walking across the gulf. He was still depressed, and very lonely: much lonelier than he had ever been that winter.

When it was daylight and he got to the mouth of Loch Fyne, he began to see tracks here and there, but most of them were old. A good many sledge tracks had been left in the fjord on the journeys between Eskimoness and Ella Island in the winter. He tried to identify a recent track among them which might be the Eskimos' sledge; but all he found were the footmarks of two men walking south. These puzzled him, because they suggested that all four of his men were not traveling together; but it was easy enough to think of explanations. Two of them might have gone on with the sledge, perhaps to gain time in taking a message through. If two were walking without a sledge, he thought he could catch them up.

Once he was in Loch Fyne, he felt more secure, both from the Germans and the weather. There was no sign that the Germans were ahead of him, and the fjord is enclosed by impassable mountains, so they could only come at him from behind; and if he saw them coming there was at least a chance in there of outwitting them by climbing the mountainside where they would not be able to follow with their sledges. As for the weather, the fjord itself gave an illusion of shelter compared with the open ice; and there were hunting huts in it, one at the mouth and one at the head and one half-way. It was twelve miles from hut to hut. He might still have been caught by a sudden storm between them, but whatever happened there was some prospect of reaching shelter in on direction or the other. Altogether, he felt more at home in Loch Fyne.

He walked on right to the head of the fjord, with only short rests in the huts on the way. Each hut gave him an attainable objective and stopped him thinking too much of the great distance still beyond. Each time he passed a hut, he put the sign of three circles on the door. At the end of a night and a day and half of another night, the first fifty miles of the journey were behind him.

In the third of the huts, at the head of the fjord, there was another portable transmitter. It was not a battery set like the one at Revet, but was powered by cranking a generator by hand. While he walked the last twelve-mile lap along the fjord, he decided to stop there and make a determined attempt to signal Scoresby Sound. It was a for-lorn hope, because the set was only a small affair which was meant to reach Eskimoness or Ella Island, and Scoresby Sound was a long way beyond its normal range. But by then he was beginning to think he would never reach Ella Island by forced marches. For one thing, he had eaten very nearly all his food. If he could get a message through, he could spend a day or two in hunting for musk-ox or arctic hare,

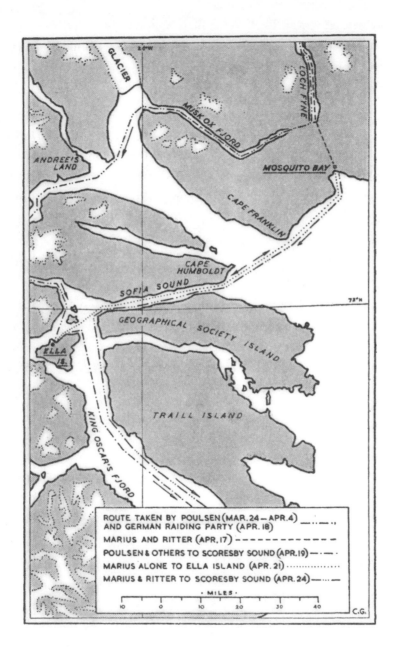

Sledge Patrol's district: middle part

and then he would have no fear of starving; but if radio contact could not be made to work, he felt he would have to press on without any delay which could possibly be avoided, and take the chance of finding enough odds and ends of food abandoned in huts along the way.

Besides food, the thing that was troubling him most by that final stage up Lock Fyne was the state of his feet. The sacks they were wrapped in were hard and coarse, and the absurdly big boots, whatever he did with them, rubbed up and down at every step. When at last he came to the hut, and had lit the stove and got some warmth in the place, he unwrapped his feet and found a disgusting mess, the toes and heels raw and bleeding, and dirt and fibres from the sacks ground into the open sores. He melted some snow in the tin and washed his feet in it, and then melted more snow in the same tin and drank it: it was no time to be fastidious. After that, he assembled the radio and waited for the time when Scoresby Sound was scheduled.

That transmitter was a most exasperating piece of machinery. It had really been designed to be operated by two people, one to turn the generator and the other to work the Morse key. Single-handed, the receiver would work all right, but the transmitter was almost impossible. At midnight, Poulsen cranked it up and heard Scoresby Sound vainly calling him at Eskimoness. When Scoresby Sound sent "over" and waited for Eskimoness to answer, Poulsen switched over to transmit, and started with all the strength he had left to try to crank with one hand and send Morse with the other. But it was no good. If he was getting a signal out at all, it was too weak for Scoresby Sound to hear it. The operator went on calling Eskimoness over and over again, and took no notice of Poulsen's frantic attempts to cut in on the wave-length. When this was added to his loneliness and weariness and pain, he could have burst out crying with frustration and self-pity. It was like a nightmare of childhood, when one is lost in a forest and can hear one's parents searching but cannot open one's mouth to answer.

He persevered with the machine for two nights and a day, in the hope that reception might be better in different conditions of daylight. He altered the crank of the generator so that he could work it with his feet and get more power behind it. But all this time was wasted. During the second night, he gave up hope of ever getting anyone to hear him; and he tool the radio out of the hut and carried it up into the hills and buried it, so that the Germans should not destroy it if they ever came that way. There was only one thing for it, and that was to go on at full speed, and even to try to make up for the time he had lost. Ad dawn, he got ready to start on his journey again, with 150 miles still to go.

From the head of Loch Fyne, there are two routes to the southward. The shortest goes due south, over a low pass, and then for 14 miles down to the sea again through a valley called the Badlands, which is a bog in summer and is full of soft snow in winter. At the foot of the Badlands is Mosquito Bay, where there is an old Norwegian weather station. From there, the route crosses the open sea-ice for forty miles to the south side of Kaiser Franz Joseph Fjord.

That route would have been difficult for a man on foot, because of the long stretch of unsheltered open sea; so Poulsen went the other way, west from the head of Loch Fyne to the head of Musk Ox Fjord, and then through the inner fjords and sounds. It is a longer route, but safer, because there are hunting huts along it all the way.

As soon as he left Loch Fyne, he got into difficult going. There is a stretch of ten miles between the heads of the two fjords, and like the Badlands valley, it is a notorious place for deep loose snow. The whole of Musk Ox Fjord is sometimes just as bad. It is the only fjord on the coast which runs in towards the ice cap, instead of out towards the sea, and it is sheltered and deep and narrow. The snow falls softly there all winter, and does not blow away. By the early spring, a man without skis would sink in it up to his middle; a skier finds it hard work, and a dog driver always expects to have to harness his team on a tandem trace and ski ahead to make them a track.

Poulsen put on his skis and carried his sleeping-bag. But the skis had no bindings which would fit his boots, and the best he could manage was a makeshift arrangement which was always on the verge of coming off. The skis sank ankle-deep in the powdery surface. The reindeer-skin sleeping bag made such a bulky awkward bundle that he gave up carrying it, and tried hauling it behind him on the snow. The ten miles overland seemed endless. Small obstacles loomed large, and he was surprised to find how difficult it was to overcome them. Before he had reached the low watershed between the fjords, he had realised that something was wrong with him, and that his usual strength appeared to have ebbed away; but it was some time later before he realised why. He was getting weaker simply because he was hungry. It was five days since he had anything that could be called a decent meal. For the last two days, he had been spinning out the remains of some oatmeal he had found in a hut in Loch Fyne, and drinking warm water. While he had stayed at the hut at the head of the lock, he had not felt the ill effects; but now, the coldness and the effort of trudging through the snow had quickly worn him out. That afternoon, he reached the first hut in Musk Ox Fjord. He had only gone 15 miles, but he could not go any farther; and that short day's march had made him admit to himself that he must get food, however long it took him to find it, because without enough to eat, in the bitter cold, he would never get to Ella Island at all.

Sometimes a man has a stroke of luck which he remembers all his life, and Poulsen never forgot that hut. It was just the same as all the others, as small and bare and sparsely furnished as any kind of human lair could be; but on a shelf in it, forgotten, he found a packet of beans. They had certainly been there for three years, and probably very much longer, ever since a pre-war hunter had stored them there on his rounds, or abandoned them there as not worth carrying away. But of course they had been frozen for three-quarters of every year, and they were still recognisable as beans. He seized them eagerly; but even then, fate gave him a last sly blow; because the beans could certainly not be eaten raw, and that hut was the first he had seen which had no fuel left in it at all. Burrowing in the snow outside, he found some old fox traps, and without a qualm of conscience he smashed them up and used them to light a fire. It might be too much to say that those beans saved Poulsen's life, but at least they made him feel well-fed that evening, and there were enough to take him the forty tedious miles down Musk Ox Fjord in the next two days.

Here and there in Musk Ox Fjord, in the neighbourhood of the huts, he could still see the same two sets of footprints which he had followed up Loch Fyne; but after the time he had wasted with the radio, he no longer hoped to catch up with the men who had made them.

At the mouth of the fjord, he got back into better country, with hard ice underfoot, among the head waters of Kaiser Franz Joseph Fjord. There he had to pass the foot of a glacier which is seven miles wide. When he had been that way before, he had thought it was the most beautiful place he had ever seen, and even now, in spite of the pain of each step that he took along the base of the wall of ice, he could still appreciate its beauty. The mountains round about are steep and high, and they are made of slanting bands of sandstone of striking colours, red and yellow and brown and a deep purple. The glacier flows so fast that one can almost see it moving, and in summer it calves enormous quantities of icebergs which sail away down the fjord. In autumn they freeze in, packed so closely in the first few miles below the glacier that in winter it is sometimes difficult to find a course between them. With a blue sky above and the diamond ice below, the place has a blazing brilliance of colour and clarity of outline which make more familiar scenes seem dingy and faded, and give the impression that this is how the new-made earth should have looked on the third morning of its creation: for the only colour which is absent is the green of life.

On the far side of the fjord, and ten miles or so below the glacier, there is a hut; and it had been well stocked with food when Poulsen had last been down that way. It was still the same; and when he got there, he had no more fear of going hungry. He sat down to an orgy there of tinned meat and oatmeal and coffee, and the thought of how long it had all been lying there did not upset him in the least.

Beyond that hut, his walk took a better turn. He was still getting weaker day by day, and the sores on his feet were deeper every evening when he washed them. But beyond a certain degree, the pain of raw feet cannot get very much worse. The weather was still fine, except for showers of snow, he had avoided serious frostbite, the ice was hard, and he was more than half-way home. The whole of the rest of the way was along the tremendous fjords of Andrée's Land; fjords five miles wide, enclosed by precipitous crags five thousand feet above the shores. The huts along their edges are spaced, as usual, ten or twelve miles apart. Each day he travelled two stages. After Musk Ox Fjord, he never weakened so much again that he could only manage one stage; but he never had the strength, as he had when he started his walk, to try to do three or four. Somewhere down there, he stalked a musk-ox. He was ashamed to kill the great beast just to satisfy himself, but he thought that fresh meat would give him more stamina. He ate a little, raw, and took a few pieces with him, and left the carcass. On April 4th, in the evening, he came within sight of the Bastion of Ella Island, a vast rock which rises behind the station there; and as he got nearer he walked out on the middle of the ice, in the hope that someone would see him and come out with a sledge to help him. He had walked 230 miles in eleven days, including the day and a half which he had wasted in Loch Fyne; and now the last five miles seemed more than he could possibly accomplish.

19

THEY DID see him from the station. When he was still some miles away, still dragging his bleeding, suppurating feet across the ice, he saw a sledge approaching. But the driver was not one of the four men whose tracks he thought he had been following, it was the Eskimo Mikael, whom he had sent south before the trouble at Eskimoness had started; and from Mikael's astonishment at seeing him, he slowly and unwillingly understood that nobody had come through from Eskimoness, and the people at Ella had not heard what had happened.

In the warmth and comfort of the house that night, Poulsen collapsed and could not even contemplate this new bewildering problem. He had known he might be mistaken about the sledge tracks, because so many people had travelled by sledge that way: but whose were the footprints he had seen so clearly? Where were his men? In his exhaustion, the past eleven days began to have the quality of a dream, and these unanswerable questions lacked reality. The men were not there: he could hardly remember why he had thought they would be: perhaps he had dreamed the footprints.

Mikael and his companion Aparte were alone, and they were terribly concerned at the state to which their leader was reduced, and at the ghastly injuries that he had done to his own feet. They fed him, and doctored him in their own rough and friendly way, and the scraps of the story which he told them grew in their imaginations to a tale of irretrievable disaster. Eskimoness captured: the leader crippled: seven men vanished: the enemy with sledges at large upon their coast. If Poulsen had been able to think at all, he would have reassured them, but the only idea which he still had in his head was the idea which had urged him on so long: to get a signal off, to tell the people outside what had been happening on the coast. He had no cypher, but he had decided long before what he would do if he got to Ella Island: he would send the signal in Eskimo, which would be just as good as a cypher because no German would understand it. He could speak Eskimo, but he could not write it; so during that evening he told the two Eskimos what he wanted to say and got them to write it down, and at midnight he raised Scoresby Sound and sent the following extraordinary signal:

FROM ELLA ISLAND

0001. APRIL 5TH

TO BRUN GODTHAAB VIA SCORESBYSOUND

2300 March 23rd Eskimoness taken by enemy in course of ten minutes. Eskimoness people escaped they have no clothes and other necessities and are separated from each other. Dog teams and code number 920 and possibly green code for

March taken by enemy I am afraid Greenland is in great danger and will perhaps be taken by the enemy if soldiers cannot come up here very soon am waiting urgently your reply because I am going on a log journey.*

This message, into which Mikael and Aparte had injected their own exaggerated fears, was translated back to Danish by Scoresby Sound and enciphered there and retransmitted to Eske Brun. But as soon as Scoresby Sound had acknowledged it, they replied with a message for Poulsen. They told him they knew about the attack on Eskimoness. Kurt Olsen had got through a short signal ten days before, on the emergency transmitter in Rudi's hut at Revet. Since then, there had been silence. On hearing this, Poulsen told Scoresby Sound to cancel the signal he had just sent, the signal which he had walked 200 miles to send; and he closed the transmitter down.

After midnight he slept, but not for very long. He did not waste much time in reflecting that most of his suffering of the past ten days had been entirely pointless, that if he had known that Kurt Olsen had used the transmitter at Revet before he got there, and had drained the last drop from the batteries in doing so, he could have taken his time about his journey and avoided reducing his feet to a bloody mess. By six o'clock in the morning, he had recovered enough to try to think ahead. He had reasoned that there was really no harm in sending an uncyphered message about something the Germans had already done; and he called Scoresby Sound again in his own language and got off a more coherent signal:

---

* Afterwards Poulsen had no recollection of having sent this signal and was embarrassed to find it on the radio station's file.

FROM ELLA ISLAND

0625. APRIL 5TH

TO BRUN GODTHAAB VIA SCORESBYSOUND

After difficult fluid situation got number two emergency transmitter going and informed of Olsen's report of 26th March. Green code number 27 with March code word and weather code number 920 captured. Suspect that green code was already known to opposition. Believe everyone present March 23rd uninjured but have lost touch with the others. Regard situation as very critical for our divided team and for the stations and supplies in the whole district. Can information be given in clear either Danish or Eskimo whether help may be expected and whether I may send further information in clear. Forced to move from present position but can probably keep regular radio contact. POULSEN.

He had added this last sentence, and the last words of the midnight signal too, because as soon as he had heard that his men had not arrived, he had made up his mind to turn round at once and go north again to look for them. He could not walk any more, even with bandages on his feet and proper socks and boots which fitted; but he thought he could take a lightly loaded sledge and ride on it. It was a matter of conscience: when a ship sinks, the captain should not be the only man who reaches shore. But he had to wait for an answer from Eske Brun; and while he was waiting, the Eskimos sighted another solitary figure on the ice: a man walking not from the north but along the shore of Ella Island, as if he had approached it from the south.

It was Evald, the Eskimo who had cried in the night in the tent on the way to Sabine Island and had been at Eskimoness when the shooting started; and when he came in and started to tell his story, it solved some of the mysteries which had been confusing Poulsen.

Evald and William had seen the tracer bullets soaring over their heads, and heard the terrifying noise of the machine-guns, and the experience had confused them so much that they had run away. There was no harm in that, because it was more or less what Poulsen had told them to do; but they had gone quite a long way before they remembered he had told them to take their sledge, and when they had come to their senses they had thought it was too dangerous to go back. Their only impulse had been to get out of the north-east coast, where things like that could happen, and go home to Scoresby Sound. So they also had started to walk, aiming not merely for Ella Island, but for home; and by the sledge route that was 400 miles away.

They had two days' start over Poulsen, because of his walk to Revet, and they had had the advantages of being properly dressed in their own clothes and of getting the first pick, such as it was, of the food in the huts on the way; and yet he had nearly caught them up. On the previous day, they had passed Ella Island, keeping as far as they could on the other side of the fjord because they were afraid the Germans might have got there; but during the night, Evald had felt ashamed of himself and decided to take the risk of going back there, so that if the Germans had not arrived he could warn the people there they might be coming. In the circumstances this was a courageous thing to do, and Poulsen appreciated it. William had gone straight on, to carry the warning, as he thought, to Scoresby Sound.

This story at least cleared up the puzzle of the footprints; but it made Poulsen even more concerned for Kurt Olsen and Henry Rudi. All the way, he had thought they were in front. Now it was clear that he had passed them somewhere right at the beginning of the walk, near Revet, and that they had been behind him ever since. The two Eskimos, as he knew to his cost, had not left much food in the huts when they had passed them, and he had finished what little there had been. Believing that all four of the others where ahead of him, and knowing that the northern party were well supplied, he had never thought of hungry men who might be coming along behind him. Kurt Olsen was young and full of vitality, and had a way of falling on his feet. Henry Rudi too was game for anything; but still, he was fifty-five. Poulsen had been depressed before: but now, waiting impatiently for the answer from Eske Brun, and exasperated by his own physical weakness, he reached new depths of self-accusation, imagining his old companion of two winters exhausted and starving among the deep snow of Musk Ox Fjord, or the empty huts of Loch Fyne.

20

THE JOURNEY had indeed been hard for Henry Rudi. On the day when Poulsen arrived at Ella Island, Rudi and Olsen, just as he had imagined them, in fact were struggling through the snow of Musk Ox Fjord and had covered rather less than half the distance.

In spite of the note which they had left at Revet, both of them knew by then that Poulsen was all right and was ahead of them on the way to Ella Island, not only because they had found his sign of three circles on the doors of the huts in Loch Fyne, but also because they had actually seen him when he left the hut at Revet.

In the fight, Rudi had fired a few aimless shots, and Olsen had fired none because he had not seen anyone to fire at. Like Poulsen, neither of them had ever seen tracer bullets before, and they were soon convinced, and rightly, that it was useless to resist. They had set off independently to Revet but had met in a narrow gorge among the hills, and they had gone on there together for the same reasons that

Poulsen had thought of: to try to make the transmitter work, and to leave a warning for the three men who were still up north.

On the day when Poulsen got to Revet and slept in the hills behind the hut, Rudi and Olsen were also sleeping, not more than a mile away. That evening, they had no reason to go down to the hut again, and as darkness fell they began to walk south along the hillside above the fjord. It was then that they saw a man walking below them on the ice, and also going south. He was too far away for them to recognise him, but there was no one it could have been but Poulsen. They thought he was making for a hut in a small fjord which opens off the head of Godthaab's Gulf, and they went there themselves in the hope of meeting him. But in the darkness, he had gone straight on across the gulf, and they never managed to catch him up again. It was by this small margin that he failed to hear that Olsen had sent his signal to Scoresby Sound.

Rudi and Olsen both had all their clothes: Rudi because he had been on watch when the Germans came, and Olsen because he had not really understood what was happening when Poulsen had shouted to him to come outside, so that he had gone into his room and dressed in a leisurely manner, while Poulsen was arguing with Ritter. In that respect, they were better off than Poulsen; and they were also not obsessed, like him, by any desperate need to hurry, except to escape from the Germans. In fact, they could not have hurried. Henry Rudi was willing and as tough as a man of fifty-five can be: but at that age, with the best will in the world, one cannot march as far or as fast on an empty stomach as a man of thirty can.

All the way round Godthaab's Gulf and along Loch Fyne, Henry Rudi had fretted that he was holding his young companion back. Because of the spacing of the huts, one had to walk either twelve miles a day or twenty-four, and Henry simply could not manage twenty-four. After the first few days, a single stage of twelve miles tired him out. His pace each day was slower than Kurt Olsen's; and while the old man trudged along as best he could, he was aware that Kurt was making an effort to hold himself in check and to pretend that even if he had been alone he would not have wanted to walk faster. All the way, especially along Loch Fyne, they were at the mercy of any whim which might have caused the Germans to explore in that direction. Each day, as they crept along, they fully expected to see the German sledges coming up behind them, and each night when they slept in huts it was only a matter of chance, so far as they knew, whether Germans would open the door and walk in before they woke.

Naturally, Henry Rudi did his best to persuade Kurt Olsen to go on ahead and leave him, inventing all kinds of specious arguments. As a matter of fact, if he had stayed in one of the huts he could probably have kept himself alive, with lucky hunting, as long as his ammunition lasted: he told Kurt Olsen he had done worse things before. But that was really beside the point, and they both knew it; because if he had stayed there, it could only have been a matter of time before the Germans picked him up. Kurt Olsen could never have thought of leaving him to his fate whatever happened. He admired the way the old man gamely struggled on, and if he ever felt impatient he was as careful as he could be not to show it.

Because there was nothing left to eat in the huts, they had to waste days in hunting. Kurt went out with his rifle, while Henry rested and kept the fires on. They kept themselves going on hares and musk-ox steak: and so, in the course of ten days, they covered some ninety miles, and got to the second hut in Musk Ox Fjord, one hut beyond the place where Poulsen had found the beans.

Once they had got out of Loch Fyne and across into Musk Ox Fjord, they had begun to worry less about the Germans. There was some reason for this. The more obvious route to the south was the direct one down by Mosquito Bay, and if the Germans did not know the country, that would be the more likely way for them to begin to explore it. But apart from that, they had felt there was a vague boundary at the head of Loch Fyne. Loch Fyne itself had felt like an enemy land: Musk Ox Fjord felt somehow more like home.

Nevertheless, Rudi and Olsen had a shock that night; for something happened which was precisely what they had expected on each of the ten nights of their journey: they heard dogs outside. They listened, and Olsen picked up his gun. Somebody had driven up with a dog sledge and stopped at the back of the hut, on the opposite side to the window. Rudi and Olsen stood listening, staring at each other, both with the same question in their minds: did the sound mean rescue, or capture? They expected German voices. They heard a man, coming round the hut towards the door, and Olsen put off his safety catch and covered the doorway. The man fumbled for the door latch, and they saw it turning, uncertainly and slowly.

The door opened and a tired voice said: "Kurt? Don't you start shooting," and the man came into the room: Peter Nielsen, whom nobody had seen for months, the man that Marius Jensen and Eli Knudsen had gone to look for away up north on Hochstetter Foreland before the fighting started.

"Peter!" Kurt Olsen said. "What happened? Are Marius and Eli with you?"

"No, they're not here," he said. "I'll tell you what happened. Eli Knudsen's dead."

21

WHEN MARIUS Jensen and Eli Knudsen had parted from Poulsen at the hunting station at Sandodden, and gone northward over the Kuppel Pass to look for Peter Nielsen, they had started to have trouble with their dogs. Eli Knudsen was driving his own team, which was well known for its speed; but Marius only had eight assorted dogs which he had borrowed at Eskimoness to replace the team he had abandoned at Cape Wynn. These eight were not a team at all. They had not been trained to work together, and there was no dog among them which was recognised as leader by the others. They fought more than usual among themselves, and drove Marius to exasperation; and Eli Knudsen was always miles ahead.

It took them three days to reach Hochstetter Foreland, and when they got to the hut where Peter had spent the winter, they found he was away; and they had to push on for another twenty miles before they came on his tracks and ran him to earth in another hunting hut.

They stayed there one night, and told him everything that had happened before they left Eskimoness: about Marius's adventure at Cape Wynn, and how Poulsen wanted them all at Eskimoness in case they had to defend the station. Eli and Marius had left Eskimoness in an atmosphere of worry and alarm. Now, discussing it all as they sat in Peter's tiny hut, so safe and peaceful and far away from all the trouble, they felt even more worried about old Henry and young Kurt, whom they had left to look after themselves in the thick of things. Between the, they tried to weigh up the risks. The journey had taken them three days longer than it should have. Poulsen had told them to come back by the route past Revet, so as to keep as far as possible from Sabine Island; but that was probably two days longer than the way they had come. There were two alternatives: either to take the route which was the safest for themselves, and leave Henry and Kurt and Poulsen alone for an extra two days, or to make a dash for it back by the Kuppel Pass and arrive to relieve the others that much earlier. It seemed to them that Poulsen was being too cautious on their behalf. The right thing to do, they all agreed, was to take a chance on Sandodden and the Kuppel Pass; and so, in spite of Poulsen's orders, they started back in that direction.

This journey also became something of a procession, with Eli Knudsen ahead and Marius and Peter lagging far behind. On the third night, they had agreed to camp on the northern side of the Kuppel Pass, so that the next day they could pass Sandodden, without going too near it, and reach Eskimoness the next evening.

However, when Marius and Peter arrived at the Pass, Eli Knudsen was not waiting there, and they saw that his tracks went on, right over the pass and down the other side. They knew he always wanted to visit Sandodden whenever he could, because it had been his own hunting station before the war, and they guessed he had gone on there; but they were tired and hungry, and so were their dogs. They were annoyed with Eli for his impatience and for not sticking to the plan they had agreed on; and when they remembered that all their food had been packed on his sledge, they were more than annoyed. All the same, they decided to camp. They found a secluded place between two steep moraines, and pitched their tent there, and spent a hungry night.

This, as it happened, was the evening of the 25th of March, the day on which Eskimoness had been reduced to ruins.

22

WHEN THE fire at Eskimoness had burnt itself out, Ritter and his men had started a fairly leisurely journey back towards Hansa Bay. On the whole, at that moment, Ritter was not displeased with himself, or with the way things had worked out. He was still somewhat worried about the men he had driven out from Eskimoness, especially Henry Rudi, and he had hated burning down the house. But, unpleasant thought it had been, he felt that nobody could say he had failed in any military duty, and he could still appease his conscience with the hope that nobody had actually been hounded to his death.

The papers he had found in the house before he burned it, especially Kurt Olsen's log book, had given him more clues about the disposition of the sledge patrol. He had got a wrong impression that it had not been Poulsen he had spoken to, but that Poulsen had already left to carry out his plan to spy on Hansa Bay, and must therefore still be somewhere round Sabine Island. He also knew that two men had gone up north to fetch another, and had probably not come back.

Being fairly certain, therefore, that there were still a few Danes in the district, he gave orders for strict precautions against surprise on the first night stop of the journey to Hansa Bay. A watch was to be kept all night, and a machine-gun mounted outside the hut which he and his party slept in. For the first stop, he chose the most convenient place: Sandodden.

The evening when they arrive there, he and his men picketed their dogs, of which they now had over fifty, out of sight among the high drifts of snow which surrounded the station, and all of the men except the sentry packed themselves into the little hut. But they had hardly settled down when the sentry called them out with a shout that a sledge was coming. The Germans seized their automatic arms and hurried out, and took up positions hidden behind the house and below the snowdrifts. They saw the sledge coming down from the Kuppel Pass and straight towards them: Knudsen driving confidently on, oblivious to danger, to visit his old hunting ground again.

Seeing that there was only one man, and that he was coming openly across the ice, Ritter told his men not to fire unless he gave the order; and when the sledge was a hundred yards away, he stepped out into view and shouted "Halt!" He saw the driver give him a startled glance, and heard him shout to his dogs and crack his whip. The dogs swerved to the right and came on, faster, and Ritter saw what the driver meant to do: for a hundred and fifty yards away was a bank of stone and snow which would have hidden the sledge if it could reach it.

"Shoot the dogs!" Ritter shouted, and as the sledge swept past the station the machine-gun opened fire. Some of the dogs in full gallop rolled over and over. The driver, riding the runners at the back of the sledge, reached down for his rifle, the machine-gun fired again, and the driver fell off the sledge face downwards in the snow and did not move. The sledge careered on, dragging dead and wounded dogs in their tangled traces.

Ritter ran out to where the driver lay, and turned him over. He was groaning thickly, and blood was in his mouth. Ritter rounded on the gunner.

"The gun jammed," the man protested. "I couldn't help it."

They carried Knudsen into the hut. Dr. Sensse was in the party, and he stripped off Knudsen's anorak and plugged the bullet wound high up in his chest; but he was unconscious, and in half an hour he died, the first man in all the recorded history of the north-east Greenland coast who had died there at the hand of a fellow man.

This sudden violent unnecessary tragedy, which began and ended in the space of a few decisive seconds, was a shock which haunted Ritter's memory for months. The other Germans also felt more or less ashamed that six well-armed men should have had to slaughter an enemy who was almost defenceless; and the gunner kept repeating his excuses. The machine-gun had jammed, he said, when he fired his first burst at the dogs, and when he had cleared the jam it had fired again before he had aimed it. One of the magazines of the gun was defective. It was simply bad luck, according to his description, that the single shot which had been in the breech had happened to kill the Dane. But for Ritter, this explanation was only the turning of the knife in the wound of his self-respect: for he had known that that gun had one defective magazine. It had been reported to him some time before, and he had given orders that the magazine should be thrown away, but he had never bothered to see that the order was carried out; and so, he told himself, his own carelessness had been an additional cause of this useless waste of life, for which in any case he, as commander of the party, was to blame.

But there was immediate action to be taken before Ritter could be alone to listen to his conscience. It was an easy guess that where one man had come down from the north, two others were likely to follow very soon; and he could not lose sight of the advantage it would give him to catch one of the Danes alive and question him. He sent some men out to drag in Knudsen's sledge and dispatch the wounded dogs and clear up the mess, and he doubled the guard and allotted posts to his men to make an ambush. There remained the question of what they should do with Knudsen's body. There was only just room for themselves in the hut, and one cannot dig a grave in frozen soil; so they carried it out and put it in a tiny shack which was built of sods close by. They were unaware of the rather ironical fact that Knudsen had built the shack himself, as a store for frozen meat, in the peaceful solitary years when he had lived there as a hunter.

When that was done, the incident was finished, in so far as it had any military significance. It was just one of those accidents which happen in war, and officially it could be covered, more or less truly, by the customary formula that the man had been shot while he was trying to escape. But in its effect on Ritter as a person and as a commander, its significance only began when the excitement had died away; and he was not the only one of the German party whose human feelings were offended; for one of them, that night or the following morning, made a wooden cross and put it on the shack, and inscribed it with Knudsen's name, which he had found from the papers in his pocket, and the words "He died for his country". Ritter never saw this emblem. If he had, the inscription might have struck him as sententious, but he could hardly have failed to see that at least one of his party, Nazi or not, had some instinct in sympathy with his own.

The next morning, when Marius Jensen came driving down from the pass, thinking about his breakfast, everything was prepared for his reception. Marius would have said he had already learned his lesson; and he would probably not have been so rash as Knudsen had been in driving up to a hut which he thought was empty without inspecting it from a distance first. But Knudsen's sledge tracks led him on, and they were obviously going to lead him to the station, and it never crossed his mind that if Knudsen had gone there the night before it might not be safe to follow him. When he saw smoke from the chimney, and a dog team picketed outside, it only made him hope that Knudsen had the frying pan on the fire, and he was within a few yards of the house when German soldiers rose up from the drifts of snow all round him and a warning burst of fire went over his head. There was nothing he could do but stop his dogs and put his hands up. The Germans searched him and took him inside the hut, and in exactly the same manner, an hour later, Peter Nielsen drove into the simple trap.

The sudden turn in their fortunes was something of a shock for Marius and Peter, and so was the news which the Germans told them of what had happened to Knudsen. Even the hunters in the sledge patrol, little though they knew of world events, had heard fearsome stories of the ruthlessness of Germans. In talking things over in the last few weeks, they had all agreed that the Germans on Sabine Island would be very unlikely to have food or time to spare for prisoners, and that if any of them were ever captured they could only expect to be shot. They had very little faith in the power of Eske Brun's arm-bands to protect them. The death of Knudsen was just the sort of thing they had expected, and as Marius and Peter were led into the hut, it was all they expected for themselves.

However, neither of them was cowed by the weapons by which they were surrounded, because neither of them had had anything to eat since the morning before, and not even the prospect of being exe-cuted could quite make them forget that they were extremely hungry. When Peter was dragged in and confronted by Ritter, he immediately asked for some breakfast. At that, the Germans began to laugh, and he and Marius were given a meagre plateful of dry oatmeal and tinned milk, which was all that the Germans had had to eat themselves.

Afterwards, Ritter began to question them. Both of them pre-tended to be much more stupid than they were, and fell back on the explanation that they were only sledge drivers and hunters, and had never been told what was going on in other parts of Greenland. Poulsen, they said, just gave them their orders, and they never asked about things that did not concern them. They did not know how many men there were at Ella Island, or how many there were in the sledge patrol. Ritter said he had heard that there were Americans at Scoresby Sound. They said there might be, for all they knew; Poulsen would never have told them a thing like that. Marius, as it happened, was able to add truthfully that he had never been there.

This pose was made easier for them both to maintain because there was an element of truth in it all. They had never been told very much because they had really lost interest in anything but their own immediate journeys, and because it was not Poulsen's or Marius's nature to talk about anything just for the sake of talking; while as for Peter, he had had nobody but his dogs to talk to for months before Marius came. It was quite true that for all they knew, a whole American army might have landed at Scoresby Sound, though both of them could have said it was very unlikely.

Ritter, being shrewder and more experienced at this sort of thing, could see through their attempts to deceive him, and he was able to make them tell him a little more than they intended, and a little more than they thought they had told him; but he could also see it was true that they knew much less than he had expected. There is nothing much that a questioner can do against studied stupidity unless he uses threats or some kind of third degree, and Ritter was too badly upset by the event of the night before to be able to contemplate more violence. Nothing he might have extracted from these prisoners seemed worth the moral effort of being tough. During the interview, he let them know he had burnt down their house, but that did not startle them into any more admissions; and he could not help adding, to relieve their anxiety and perhaps to excuse himself, that so far as he knew their friends had all got away. After an hour or so of interrogation, he left Marius and Peter under guard in the hut and went outside alone.

Some of Ritter's men had noticed that he seemed distraught, and had spoken about it among themselves: and in fact, the past twelve hours had been a turning point in his life. It is more than likely that some of his companions would have sympathised with his feelings, especially perhaps the man who made the cross; but he could not discuss his feelings with them. A commander does not confide such personal matters in the men he has been appointed to command; and besides, if Ritter had invited sympathy from one of his men, he would only have been inviting that man into the same intolerable position in which he found himself, and perhaps even dragging another family into the nightmare of Gestapo suspicion and revenge. He had to face his moral struggle all alone, without any benefit of human sympathy or advice.

The fact was that by all the standards Ritter had been brought up to respect, the killing of Knudsen was a crime and a sin, and seeing it done before his eyes, he could not believe that any consideration of politics could excuse it. Of course, it had been an accident; but the crime lay in the circumstances which had made him bring weapons of war to the arctic and invade a hunter's hut and lie in wait for him and threaten him when he came there. The sin was that he had ever accepted a job which in any way served a system he abhorred. Ritter perceived, as he stood outside the hut at Sandodden that March morning, the old truth that a man may never compromise with evil. Back in Germany, it had seemed wise to take that fortunate chance to go to the arctic again, for the sake of his own security and his family's. But evil had caught him up, as it will always catch a man who fails to grapple it. Now, in the light of the arctic spring, so brilliant and clear both in fact and in metaphor, he could see what a dreadful mistake he had made, and where it had led him. Knudsen had had every human right to come in peace that evening to his hut, and Ritter himself had had none. The Danes and Norwegians and Eskimos had a right to their harmless existence in Greenland, and he, through his own compromise, had become the invader and aggressor and disturber of the ancient arctic peace. Marius and Peter were simple straightforward people, like other ordinary people he had known in Austria and Czechoslovakia and Norway and Spitsbergen, and in Germany itself, the kind of people who had always been his friends. It was proper that people like them, from any nation, should act together in opposition to evil wherever it might happen to arise, and it would have been right for him to have acted with them.

To have admitted this belief had been difficult, but to act on it was far more difficult still. One man cannot start a revolution. Ritter could have made a dramatic gesture when he got back to Hansa Bay, and assembled his men and told them what he believed; but that would have had only one result. He would have had to give up his command, and submit to some kind of imprisonment. The Nazi faction would have been strengthened, and it could only have done more harm than good to everyone else, Germans and Danes alike. It would not have put right the wrong he had done already, and it would certainly have brought down revenge on his wife and daughter.

All he could think of to do was to make one definite resolution, and he made it that morning: he would not allow this crime to be repeated. If it came to the test again, he would pray to be guided by Christian, not Nazi principles, whatever the consequences might be; if his wife had to suffer for it then, she would understand; and in the meantime, he could only wait and see what the next few weeks would bring, and try to keep his secret to himself.

Sandodden had become a hateful place for him, and he gave orders to journey on. The Germans harnessed their dogs and drove away, taking their prisoners with them, and peace and quietness settled again on this scene of violence. The remains of Knudsen were left lying in the shack beside the hut; and they still lie there to-day.

23

THE GERMANS had captured every single dog which had been at Eskimoness, except the one they had shot, and part of Knudsen's team
from Ella Island too. They now had the makings of eight teams, and
they could only take them all back to Sabine Island if they let Peter
and Marius drive one each. Ritter divided this cavalcade into two parties for the rest of the journey, and sent Peter with the first while he
and Marius travelled with the second. One party went south along
the shore of Wollaston Foreland, and the other north over the Kuppel
Pass, to approach Sabine Island from the other side. Ritter, believing
that Poulsen was somewhere round the island, hoped by this means
to pick up his tracks and catch him. In spite of every thing, he would
have liked to interrogate Poulsen.

Before they left Sandodden, the prisoners were told that if one of
them gave trouble on the journey, or tried to escape, or gave any help

to Poulsen, the other one would be punished. They were not told what the punishment would be, but it was a threat which they had to take seriously.

However, Ritter took all the sting out of the threat for Marius by giving him back his old team, the one he had lost at Cape Wynn. Marius was surprised at this quite unexpectedly sympathetic gesture, and rather suspected there might be a catch in it; but anyhow, he was very glad to see his dogs again. He had lived with them all through the winter and known each one of them well, and he had missed them almost as much as he would have missed human friends; it had not been the same at all to drive the unfamiliar lot he had had to borrow. He and the dogs had an affectionate reunion, and Ritter watched it.

After Peter and the first three men had gone, something else happened which helped to raise Marius's spirits. Ritter told two Germans of the second party to start, and they both called to their dogs to go and set off with a practised air. After a few seconds, one team caught sight of the other out of the corners of its eyes, and at once the two orderly teams disintegrated into a tangled mass of snapping, yelping dogs, the sledges collided and overturned and one of the most comprehensive dog-fights even Marius had ever seen was under way. The two German drivers, mixed up in it at first, extracted themselves and hovered on the fringes of the mob. Ritter and Marius watched them in silence for a while, and then Ritter told Marius to go and sort them out. Marius ran to the sledges and waded in and laid about him with an expert hand, and very quickly the dogs understood his bad language and recognised that this was somebody who knew what he was doing, and they separated, panting and pleased with themselves.

Nothing, of course, except escape, can please a prisoner more than to see his captors in a thoroughly undignified position. To discover that the Germans were far from efficient at the all-important art of driving dogs immediately restored Marius's self-confidence. He understood for the first time why they had failed to follow him from Cape Wynn, and he began at once to think about escaping.

During the first day's journey, as it happened, he had at least two possible chances to get away. The first was when the Germans saw a musk-ox. They set off to stalk it, leaving one man alone to guard him; and while the others were away, the guard discovered he had put an American cartridge in his sub-machine gun and it had stuck in the breech. At that moment, Marius could almost have walked away. The second chance came when Ritter and Marius were driving alone, some distance from the others, and a heavy fall of snow came down. Ritter, so far as Marius could see, was only carrying a revolver, and visibility was less than fifty yards. With a quick turn and a shout to his well-trained dogs, Marius would have only run a small risk from the revolver, and he could have been sure to outdistance any pursuit by the time the snow had stopped. But on both these occasions, he was deterred by the threat to Peter; and in any case, when he came to think of it, it was not much use to give in to the temptation merely to get out of the Germans' hands. He was imprisoned by something much more effective than German weapons, and that was distance. He had no food on his sledge, and more important still, no dog food, and of course he had no rifle. With nothing for the dogs to eat, and no means of hunting, he could not get far away and would only starve.

Marius and Ritter and their party caught up with Peter and the others when they all came to Germania Harbour: the very place where all the trouble had started. There Peter and Marius were left under guard, while Ritter and most of the Germans went on to the base which Marius now knew for certain was hidden in Hansa Bay.

For Marius and Peter, a most curious kind of imprisonment began. Ritter knew there was no need for him to lock his prisoners up. He had no inclination to give them the ruthless treatment he guessed they had expected, and he picked the older men of his trawler crew, rather than the Nazis, to look after them. The hut was small, and the guard had no option but to live on terms of equality with the prisoners.

It is a well-worn saying that the common people of any nation get on quite well together whenever they are left to themselves to do so, and it is usually true; and it happened again at Germania Harbour. The German sailors, at the end of their first winter in the arctic, were glad of the chance to pick up tips about arctic crafts from the experienced Danish hunters. The two Danes were surprised to find that the Germans did not behave like the fiends that everyone had told them to expect. Although they could not understand very much of each other's language, there was no getting away from the fact that they had a lot of interests in common. One of them was hunting. One morning, when they saw a bear on the ice some distance away, the hunting instinct got the better of them all. The Germans knew that Marius was more likely to get the bear than they were, and so they lent him a rifle; and he had the unusual experience of stalking the bear while a German with a sub-machine gun, at a discreet distance behind, stalked him. He shot the bear, but it was on one of the stretches of thin ice which are found off the south of Sabine Island. The ice broke, and the dead bear fell through, and they lost it. They all grieved together over this bit of bad luck.

But although their captivity was quite comfortable and even had its enjoyable moments, and their expectation of a firing squad soon faded, Peter and Marius plotted from the very beginning to get away. Now that Eskimoness did not exist, the only place they could escape to was Ella Island, and it was no use escaping at all without a sledge and a rifle. The whole problem was how to steal or otherwise extract these things from the Germans. Marius had always believed, or pretended to believe, that Peter was a poor sledge driver, though as a matter of fact if there was any difference between them it was only in the refinements of the art and not in the distance they could travel. So the essence of all the plans that Marius thought of was to get Peter away first. He set to work to implant in the Germans' minds, just in case it should come in useful, the idea that even if Peter was let loose with a sledge and all he wanted, he would never be able to get to Ella Island alone. He said Peter had never been south of Eskimoness and was notorious for having no sense of direction, that there was no food in the huts to the southward and very little hunting, and that the farther south one went the worse the sledging conditions would become. Really, he was quite confident that if he could only get Peter well away, he would soon be able to find a chance to follow him, and that if Peter did get stuck on the way to Ella, he could pick him up before he got into trouble. Between them, in the course of a few days, they thought out a naïve and simple scheme.

24

RITTER, IN those few days, was at Hansa Bay. To some extent, as soon as he had clearly stated to himself his own fundamental disagreement with Nazi aims, he had found it easier to deal with Schmidt and his companions. He was also helped by Schmidt's attitude about what had happened on the journey. Ritter did not give Schmidt much chance to express his feelings, if he had any, about the death of Knudsen; but he expected some sign of Nazi approval of the burning of Eskimoness. But Schmidt did not seem to approve. On the contrary, he gave the impression that he thought it a pity to have destroyed such an excellent house, and implied that it was this kind of excess which was bound to alienate the people whom it was the German mission to protect. Ritter realised anew that Schmidt had already condemned him in his own mind. Burning down the house had done no good. If he had left it standing, the Nazis would have blamed him for neglect of duty; because he had burned it, they regarded his act as an unnecessary provocation of the Danes. Whatever he had done, and whatever he did in future, it would be wrong in Nazi eyes, and they would be able to twist it into another ground for accusation. Therefore, he could give up any effort to appease them. At last, he could give up looking at everything he did with a view to defending it in a court in Germany, because he was convinced at last that when his trial came, as he supposed it must, he was certain to be condemned. His self-examination had given him moral courage, and even when he was back at Hansa Bay, he could still clearly see the only course before him. All that was left for him was to try to do God's will; and if it should be God's will, so to conduct himself that whatever he himself might have to suffer at Gestapo hands, his wife and daughter might be spared.

The first of the problems which he faced with this new purpose was the problem of his prisoners. He was able to think more logically than he had for some months past. Even a week before, he might have been tempted to treat the prisoners as he imagined Schmidt would think they should be treated, and to make sure that everything he did with them could be clearly explained in ordinary military terms. But now, he was able to use his common sense. On the journey, he had admired Marius's expert handling of his dogs, though he had been careful not to show it, and he had thought how extremely useful it would be to have a first-class sledge driver to teach his own men. With eight teams, and enough competent men to drive them, he could have moved all his men, and enough food and equipment to keep them alive, and perhaps even the radio transmitters and meteorological apparatus; and so they might have been able to dodge the American bombing which he still expected day by day, and even hold out till the thaw came and the *Sachsen* was unfrozen. With this idea half-formed in his mind, he went back to Germania Harbour, and asked Marius if he was willing, during his captivity, to train the Germans and act as a kind of pilot.

Marius refused; but he used the opportunity of this talk with Ritter to try the plan which he and Peter had thought out. He appealed to Ritter to let Peter take a dog team and go back to Sandodden to make a proper job of burying Knudsen. He told Ritter how much he and Peter had disliked the idea of their companion's body being left unprotected from the foxes, and of course it was true that they did. Also, he said again that Peter was such a second-rate driver that he would not be able to escape; and although this was not true, Marius half believed it. But Ritter refused, and they parted without having settled anything.

When Ritter got back to Hansa Bay, he thought over what Marius had suggested. He had not quite been deceived by Marius's display of innocence. He thought that if he let Peter go as far as Sandodden, he would probably try to escape, and he suspected that Peter could not be quite so incompetent as Marius had pretended. The question was whether it really mattered if he escaped or not. Prisoners of war are always more or less a liability to their captors, and the only reason for keeping them in captivity is to stop them fighting again. Even if Peter got away, and succeeded in getting to Ella Island and was fitted up with a new rifle when he got there, one rifleman hundreds of miles away would only make a negligible difference to the strength of an opposition which included the American Air Force. On the other hand, as long as he stayed where he was, he had to be guarded, if only for form's sake, and he ate a man's ration of food.

Thinking further, Ritter reasoned that if Peter was allowed to go to Ella, he would be certain to tell the rest of the sledge patrol that the Germans were well armed and well organised, and that this warning might help to deter them from trying an attack on Hansa Bay, or searching for his base again if he managed to move it.

A day or two later, Ritter and Marius had another meeting. By then, each of them had decided in his own mind to make a bargain; and in the upshot, Marius agreed to pilot Ritter on a reconnaissance northward towards Hochstetter Foreland, and Ritter agreed in return to let Peter go to Sandodden; and he told him to wait there, when he had done what he wanted to do with Knudsen's burial place, until a German party came to fetch him back.

When Schmidt and the other Nazis heard of these plans, their feelings ran high. They had only thought of the prisoners, if they thought at all, on orthodox lines, and to let one of them go alone on a long journey seemed to them the worst depth of incompetence to which Ritter had yet sunk. But Ritter shrugged his shoulders, and did not bother to tackle the hopeless task of trying to explain his reasoning; he merely pretended that as he had told Peter to stay at Sandodden, he expected his order to be obeyed. Schmidt thought he was being a credulous fool. But by then, Schmidt and Ritter never spoke to each other if they could help it, and the question was not discussed between them.

At about this time, Dr. Weiss the meteorologist put forward a plan of his own. He wanted to go, with Dr. Sensse and a few of the best of the German sledge drivers, and drive right down to Ella Island, and do there what Ritter had done at Eskimoness: namely, put the place out of action as a weather station. The reasons for doing this were less convincing than they had been at Eskimoness, because Ella Island was too far away to give local reports of the Sabine Island weather to the American Air Force. Ritter suspected that what Weiss and Sensse really wanted, now that they had more or less learnt the art of driving dogs, was the pleasure of a really long arctic journey, as an experience to remember in future years. Ritter could not help sympathising with that, and he agreed with the plan. He had an added reason for welcoming the proposal; for one of the men Weiss wanted to take was Schmidt. The journey would take several weeks; for the base, it promised several weeks of peace from internal strife.

So preparations were started for three journeys from Sabine Island. Peter was given a small team of six dogs, and enough provisions to take him to Sandodden and keep him there for a few days. Ritter was getting ready to travel with Marius on his reconnaissance to the northward; and Weiss and Sensse, with the help of Schmidt and two others, unknown to Marius or Peter, were fitting out sledges for an attack on Ella Island. Peter was the first of them to start.

The commanders: Poulsen's first meeting with his "General," Eske Brun, on their return to Denmark at the end of the war

Lieutenant Ritter

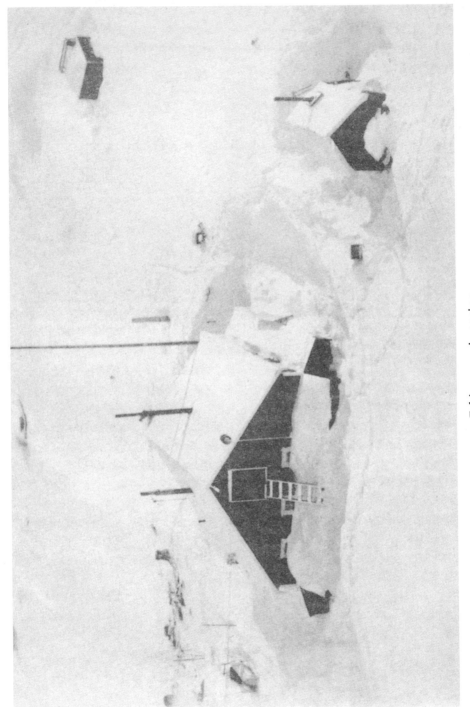

Eskimoness in spring

Henry Rudi

Kurt Olsen and Marius Jensen at the end of the war

The Sledge Patrol. On hard ice the team is harnessed in a fan: one man has jumped on the sledge, still wearing his skis.

In the soft snow, the dogs are on a tandem trace, and one man skis ahead to make a track. The picture was taken at midnight in May in King Oscar's Fjord.

Carlsberg Fjord on
the sledge route to
Scoresby Sound

Three of the Patrol's teams at the start of a blizzard: the dogs lie curled up till the
snow drifts over them.

Sandodden. The shack where Knudsen was buried and the cross which the Germans made

Marius Jensen's team, which he lost at Cape Wynn and got back at Sandodden, with the hills of Clavering Island across the sound

Poulsen and two of the Sledge Patrol Eskimos

Ella Island in summer

Scoresby Sound in spring, looking west towards Hurry Inlet

25

THIS WAS how it had come about that Peter came driving down the way to Ella Island all alone, and caught up with Henry Rudi and Kurt Olsen on their weary journey through Musk Ox Fjord. He had been to Sandodden, and hastily grubbed up stones and heaped them over the shack where Knudsen lay, and he had exchanged the sledge which the Germans had given him for a lighter one which had been left there; and he had set off again without wasting a minute, or giving a thought to Ritter's half-hearted order that he should wait there till the Germans came to fetch him. For Henry and Kurt, his arrival saved the situation. They all went on together, taking turns to ride on Peter's sledge, but giving the lion's share of the rides to Henry.

But meanwhile, at Ella Island, there was still no news of what had become of them, and Poulsen's anxiety was increasing day by day. As things had turned out, he had had to put off his plan to go north to look for the missing men. When Eske Brun had heard the first brief news of the capture of Eskimoness, from the signal which Kurt Olsen had managed to send from Revet, he had made up his mind at once what he ought to do; and what he had done was to tell the senior man in the sledge patrol at Scoresby Sound to go north at full speed to Ella to give what help he could, and to take with him all the forces he could muster. Poulsen now heard by radio that this man, whose name was Ziebell, was already well on the way, and had rounded up no less than eight sledges driven by Eskimo volunteers. This must have been the largest body of men and dogs which had ever gone north from the settlement and travelled up the colossal barren length of King Oscar's Fjord. It would have been senseless for Poulsen to have set off to look for his men alone when this number of searchers was on the way; it was much better to wait till they arrived, and then to organise the search on a scale that was likely to succeed. So he had to curb his anxiety and impatience. As a matter of fact, it was just as well that this delay was forced on him, because although he would not have admitted it, he was too ill to travel safely. Apart from his feet, he was covered with half-healed frostbite sores, and he was so tired that several days of rest were what he needed. If he had started impetuously straight away, he would have been simply asking for disaster.

While he waited, Poulsen himself was in a vulnerable position. The house at Ella Island he knew would be the Germans' first important objective, if they were bent on ravaging the coast, and he, a sick man, was sitting in it with three rather nervous Eskimos and only one sledge between the four of them. So on the day after he got there, he sent two of the Eskimos, with the sledge, to set up a depot on the south side of the island, the opposite side to the house. They put up tents and stored some food in them, together with the station's portable emergency transmitter; and the next day all four of the men drove round there, along the foot of the sheer 4000-foot cliffs which make the island a landmark, and they left the station empty. By climbing the hills of the island, they could look down on the station without being seen themselves, and keep a watch on the ice for a good distance to the northward.

However, while they were driving round the west side of the island, Ziebell and his squadron of Eskimos were actually driving round it from the east, at the end of a forced march over the couple of hundred miles from Scoresby Sound; and Ziebell, finding the house still warm and fresh tracks leading out of it, sent five of the Eskimos in pursuit. These men followed the tracks to the depot, and got there just after Poulsen had unpacked his sledge. In a hurried exchange of news, it turned out that one of the five was the brother of William, the Eskimo who had walked down from Eskimoness and, so far as anyone knew, was still on his way to Scoresby Sound on foot; and this man left at once for the south again to try to catch up with William and help him home. The other four, with Poulsen's three Eskimos, settled down at the depot, while Poulsen harnessed some dogs again and drove back to the station, anxious to meet Ziebell.

This meeting was a tonic which Poulsen badly needed. He had not seen anyone he could really talk to since Eskimoness. Everything had seemed to him to be dissolving into chaos and disaster, and his own responsibility for it had seemed almost more than he could bear. It is always when things go wrong that one most needs a friend to point out that things might have been worse; and Ziebell was an excellent person for the job of cheering Poulsen up: unruffled and humourous, and with the civilised and urbane point of view which was appropriate in a man from Scoresby Sound. He was also, for what it was worth, the only other officer in the Greenland Army.

However, he had brought new orders from Eske Brun which were not very welcome. As soon as everyone possible had been gathered in to Ella Island, they were to retreat to Scoresby Sound to defend the settlement. This was another blow to Poulsen's self-esteem, but he had to admit that like all the governor's orders it was a matter of common sense. Poulsen, still smarting from his defeat at Eskimoness, had been thinking of leading a party north for his revenge; but so long as the sledge patrol was campaigning up the coast, there would be nobody to resist a surprise attack on Scoresby Sound; and Scoresby Sound, with its homesteads and radio station and peaceful people, was the only place on the coast which was really worth defending. If the Germans were left alone away up in the north, there was nothing they could do except destroy a lot of hunting huts and perhaps the station at Ella. There would not be any loss of life, and the Americans would come along and deal with them in the end. No commander in the field likes to be told to give ground when he still feels able to defend it; but this was a clear case for what is called a strategic withdrawal.

The arrival of Ziebell was doubly fortunate, because Ella Island, in the next few days, fell into a state of complete confusion. During the night at the depot, Ziebell's Eskimos and Poulsen's had talked things over. Evald's story of the tracer bullets and the downfall of Eskimoness, in passing from mouth to mouth, had had horror upon horror added to it; and in the morning all the Eskimos with one accord announced that they were going back to Scoresby Sound at once.

The Eskimos must not be blamed for this, or for any of their other inconvenient decisions, and it must not be thought they were cowards, for they were not. But Scoresby Sound and the empty coast were the whole of their world, and beings whom so far they had never seen, armed with mysterious weapons, had appeared in it from a land they had never heard of. It was just as if creatures in flying saucers had really descended, with death rays and warlike intentions, on a peaceful American or European village; and judged by that true comparison, the Eskimos' reactions were probably normal. After a first panic they wanted to go home, to die with their families.

All the same, it was awkward for Poulsen, who wanted them to come north with him to find the missing men, and only then to retreat in good order to the south. He and Ziebell spent most of the next two days in arguing and explaining and persuading, all in the

Eskimo language, while the Eskimos argued among themselves and all talked at once and hardly had any time to listen. Rumours flourished quickly and died away. Opinion veered back and forth, influenced by every fresh suggestion. It received its worst setback when somebody pointed out that it was not only the five men from Eskimoness who were missing; for two Norwegian brothers called Akre had been based at Ella Island, and had been away on a patrol round Geographical Society Island, and should have been back by then. Because they were late, it was only too easy to jump to the conclusion that they had been captured, and that therefore the Germans were only just round the corner, perhaps choosing their moment to attack, perhaps watching the station from the mountains across the fjord. As this idea gained ground, it became impossible to hold back the remaining men who had volunteered, and four of them set off full speed for home, with empty sledges to enable them to travel all the faster. Two of the men from Eskimoness, Mikael and Evald, were sent with them by Poulsen, because they had lost their sledges to the Germans and were no use to him without them.

That left four who had proved to be more resolute than the rest: two called Lars and Christian, who had been members of the sledge patrol in Scoresby Sound and had not just volunteered for this special journey; Aparte, the last of the four from Eskimoness; and a revered old hunter from Scoresby Sound with the good old-fashioned arctic name of Josva Barselaisen, who had refused to be stampeded by any of the arguments and was simply not afraid of anything. These four had agreed to come two days' journey north with Ziebell and Poulsen; but no sooner had their decision been made than a signal came from Scoresby Sound with the sad news that Josva's only son had been killed in an accident. So he also had to go, and he took Aparte with him; and then there were two.

While the last echoes of this tremendous discussion were still dying away, three of the men who had been the crux of it came driving in to

Ella in good heart: Peter Nielsen, Henry Rudi and Kurt Olsen, all on Peter's sledge; and immediately for at least the tenth time in five days, the entire situation changed again.

Peter had reached Musk Ox Fjord in four days from Sabine Island, and taking the other two men with him he had got to Ella Island in four days more, a total distance of about 270 miles. With only six dogs, this was a remarkable achievement by any standards, and should have put an end to Marius's scorn about his driving.

He brought Poulsen a tremendous amount of news: the first news that Eskimoness had been burnt down after it was captured, the news of Eli Knudsen's death and his own and Marius's capture, and above all the first definite confirmation that the German base was in Hansa Bay, and a fairly accurate idea of the number of men in it and the kind of armament they had.

All this was information which had to be sent to Eske Brun; but the only code which Poulsen had at Ella was the one called the green code. This was the code which had been in use at Eskimoness before the attack began. Ever since the Germans' shouts across the ice had shown that they knew exactly who was in the house, Poulsen had believed that they had broken this code and had been able to read his signals. Anyhow, a copy of it had been left behind in the house when it was captured, so it was certainly unsafe to use it now. He therefore made up his mind to send more sledges south, to take Peter's news in writing to Scoresby Sound. This meant a delay of six days or so in getting the information out, but that seemed better than the risk of letting the Germans know that Peter had come safely through with it. In fact, Poulsen and Peter thought a few days' delay might be just as well. They thought the Americans might be waiting for more definite information than the sledge patrol had been able to send out, and that this new instalment might be all they needed for an immediate smashing blow on Sabine Island. But the attack had been delayed so long already that a few days more did not seem to matter very much, and every day, they reckoned, would give Marius another chance to get away before the place was bombed.

Luckily, although Josva and Aparte had already gone when Peter and the others came in, they had only got as far as the reserve depot on the south side of the island, and Poulsen was able to catch them before they left there. On the next day, April 10th, he sent them off with light sledges to travel fast and carry his dispatch; and behind them, with two more sledges, went Lars and Christian, Peter, Henry and Kurt Olsen. Poulsen borrowed Christian's sledge and team; and he and Ziebell stayed behind at Ella to cover the retreat.

It was nearly a week since Poulsen had finished his walk. Because he was young and remarkably healthy, none of his sores had gone gangrenous and most of them had healed themselves already. Now that he had the encouraging company of Ziebell, he was almost himself again. The Ghastly muddle and confusion of the last six days was sorted out at last, and with good dogs and one reliable companion he felt he could cope with anything that could happen at Ella Island. One of his men was dead, but only three were still missing. There was really no reason to think that the two Norwegian brothers from Ella Island had run into serious trouble, and they had everything they needed to get back to Scoresby Sound alone. The only man he was very worried about was Marius Jensen, still in the Germans' hands.

26

MARIUS HIMSELF was not very seriously worried, except through knowing how Poulsen would worry on his behalf; but he was puzzled. On that same day, the 10th of April, he was right up on Hochstetter Foreland, 300 miles away from the nearest of his friends, alone with the German commander; and he could not understand why the German had taken him there, or what he was looking for so far to the northward.

Quite possible Ritter himself, on that day, could not have explained what had made him take his prisoner, without any of his own men, on that journey so far into the perfect desolation of the ultimate northeast. When he started, he had had a definite objective: to investigate the hunting stations within reach of Sabine Island, and to see if any of them could house his men and his equipment in case they had to move from Hansa Bay. But something strange had happened as soon as he got away from Hansa Bay and its horrible associations, and away from the atmosphere, so foreign to the arctic, of sordid mistrust and mad politics. Suddenly, as if he had woken from a nightmare, everything was exactly as it had been in his happy Spitzbergen years. Once again, he was free, in the incomparable arctic freedom; again he was lapped in the God-given beauty of the arctic scene; and again he heard the ring of sledge runners and the eager belling of well-trained dogs in the hands of an expert driver, the very sound of freedom, and knew that his own word would direct them where he wished, to stop or to journey on, to rest or to hunt. He was like a man come home from exile, or released from a sentence of death, and all the commonplace details of an arctic journey filled him with new delight.

He and Marius travelled together across the upheaval of the pressure ice to the north of Sabine Island, and out over Hochstetter Bay till the tops of the hills of Sabine sank at last below the south horizon, and they entered fastnesses where Ritter had never been before, tremendous tracts of fjord and ice and mountain which even now only a handful of men have ever seen, and which never have been disturbed by the faintest echo of war. Neither of them spoke very much on their journey, even at night, in huts or in the tent, when the dogs had been fed and the two men cooked and ate together and shared the chores and slept within an arm's length of each other. Marius at any time was a taciturn man; and Ritter could not have found words to express his ecstatic feeling, even when he quite forgot, as he often did, that Marius was his prisoner and not only his companion. But when they spoke, Marius spoke Danish and Ritter Norwegian. Ritter was thinking again in Norwegian, instead of in German; and that served to complete his illusion that the horrible events of the past few months had been a dream, and to make him feel that now, in those blessedly impersonal surroundings, he could be himself again, the man he had been born and brought up to be; for the man he had become, the Ritter who had plotted and lied and burned and laid a lethal trap for a hunter, seemed a stranger he could hardly recognise.

In this curiously twisted frame of mine, Ritter had a single mad desire: to go on north, away from Sabine Island and away from humanity, to travel on and on across the endless ice which stretched unbroken to the north pole and beyond it, to travel on and never to come back.

If a psychoanalyst had been watching Ritter in the first days of that pilgrimage, he might have diagnosed a nervous breakdown; but Marius was no psychoanalyst, and he could never possibly have guessed the stresses which had forced his captor to the edge of a temporary madness. He saw that the German commander was unpredictable in his decisions, and very often inclined to change his mind. When Ritter asked him if it was possible to travel right up to the north of Greenland, and round the north coast and down towards Baffin Island and Hudson's Bay, he hardly took the question seriously, and told him two men and one sledge could never make such a journey. But what surprised him most was that Ritter was so unlike what he had expected a German commander to be. There was none of the harshness which everyone had talked about, and not even much of the ruthless efficiency; instead, he seemed to be a vague and gentle, friendly person whose only wish was to talk about his family in Austria and to learn all there was to know about driving dogs. Marius would perhaps have been even more surprised if he had known that Ritter really liked him and was enjoying his company and found even his long silences endearing, because they were so typical of all the arctic hunters he had known.

For about ten days this ill-matched but strangely congenial pair drove aimlessly here and there about the huts in the distant north, which were deserted since Peter had left the district. Marius began to get a little impatient at the delay of his plans to escape. There was no lack of chances to escape. As the escort of a prisoner, Ritter was being completely careless; but Marius could not bring himself to take advantage of him. He had promised to drive him on this journey, in return for permission for Peter to go to Sandodden, and he could not break his promise, provided the journey did not go on for ever. Besides, he could only have escaped by killing Ritter or leaving him alone up there to die. They only had one sledge between them. Ritter had one rifle and one revolver, and Marius had none. To journey south again, the sledge and the rifle were essential: the revolver was a useless weapon when it came to hunting. Marius could have stolen the rifle and driven the sledge away, but then Ritter would have starved; or of course he could have shot Ritter in his sleep. Perhaps, by warlike standards, it was Marius's duty as a prisoner to kill Ritter and get away, and congratulate himself on having rid his country of an enemy; but Marius did not know much about the duties of a prisoner of war, and it never seriously occurred to him to do it; while if Ritter ever thought about it at all in his trance of delusive happiness, he knew by an intuition that Marius would never do him any harm if he could help it.

But although the sudden shock of freedom had been the final cause which almost pushed Ritter over the edge of reason, freedom was also his cure. Slowly, as the perfectly peaceful days passed by, he began to think in a balanced way again, and to remember that he still had more to do than to die or to run away. He was able to pray; and as his reason began to reassert itself, he saw that the impulse to go farther and farther north was only a renewal of the impulse he had felt at Eskimoness, to look for a death without a deliberate suicide; for deliberate suicide was an act which his temperament and his religion made impossible, however welcome the restfulness of death might be. To go on and on to the northward had appealed to him because it had a melodramatic fitness; but sooner or later, he and Marius would have come to a point of no return, and when they came to that point he would not really have wanted to drag Marius beyond it. If suicide had really been any solution, he only needed to order Marius to leave him where he was, to take the sledge and the rifle, and perhaps to leave the revolver. Certainly his body would never be found again, and if any of his men still wanted to think the best of him, they might put down his disappearance to an accident, or guess that Marius had killed him. But he could not expect such a charitable judgment from the Nazis. They would be more likely to put him down as a deserter, and add that to the crimes for which his wife would suffer.

Besides, he had really intended to find somewhere safe for his men to shelter while the Americans bombed Hansa Bay, or at least somewhere for survivors to retire if the bombing entirely destroyed the base and made it uninhabitable. Suddenly and inconsequently, about the 12th of April, he realised how much time he had already wasted in his search, and he came abruptly to his senses and was filled with remorse. At once he told Marius to turn and drive him south again. Marius said nothing, but did as he was told.

They went down by way of the Kuppel Pass, without going to Hansa Bay; and then, avoiding Sandodden with its sinister memories and its frozen corpse still lying in the outhouse, they turned inland and went to Revet. Then Ritter directed Marius farther south, into the mouth of Loch Fyne. In the lock, as they drove hurriedly along it, there were two new sledge tracks going south imposed on the snow which had fallen within the last few days. Each of them speculated in silence about these tracks.

All through this rapid southward journey, Marius still held his hand and made no effort to escape, but now his reason was a new one: there was no point in escaping from Ritter so long as Ritter ordered him to drive at top speed in the direction he wanted to go. He merely wondered anew what Ritter was planning.

As they went down Loch Fyne, the weather began to break. All through that early spring, it had been stable, with nothing worse than scattered showers of snow; but among the mountains of Loch Fyne and Hold With Hope a strong wind was blowing and heavy snow was falling on the day when Ritter and Marius approached them. As they went on, into the heart of the area of the storm, conditions became extremely difficult; but Ritter urged Marius on, past the hut in the middle of the loch, and past the hut where Poulsen, a fortnight before, had tried in vain to make the radio work. Here, at the head of the loch, all the old sledge tracks turned west towards Musk Ox Fjord; but the two new ones, only visible here and there where an eddy of wind had kept the ice swept bare, led on to the southward, towards the Badlands Valley and towards Mosquito Bay. At the hut where the ways divided, Ritter at last told Marius where he was heading, and ordered him to press on to Mosquito Bay. He had seen the hunting stations at Hochstetter Foreland, Sandodden and Revet: Mosquito Bay was the last within range of Sabine Island as a possible retreat.

So Marius led on, across the watershed and down the valley through the deep heavy snow. He was sure the tracks he had seen would lead to the station, and they were so new that whoever had made them would probably still be there, sheltering from the storm. He tried to reason out whose tracks they could possibly be: not Peter's, because he had been travelling alone, and not Poulsen's or Henry's or Kurt's, because they had been made long after those three had been driven south. But whoever had made the tracks, Marius knew he would have to follow them to the station. The Badlands Valley was a kind of cul-de-sac. In a northerly gale, it was impossible to think of driving beyond the end of it, out across the forty miles of sea-ice at its foot, and impossible also to turn and drive up it again with the wind ahead. The hut at Mosquito Bay was the only shelter he could hope to reach.

They were quite close to the hut before he saw it through the driven snow. He saw dogs outside it and recognised them; and he cursed himself for having left his escape too late, for they were dogs which the Germans had captured. As he and Ritter drove up to the house, it was Schmidt, with a sub-machine-gun in his hand, who made them welcome.

27

THE WHOLE of Dr. Weiss's party was in the house, and probably they were just as surprised at this meeting as Ritter or Marius himself. It was surprising enough to see two travellers emerging from the storm, because they themselves, on their way to make their attack on Ella Island, had been storm-bound in Mosquito Bay for nearly a week; but it was doubly surprising, when the two men raised their heads so that their faces were no longer hidden by the hoods of their anoraks, to recognise Ritter and his prisoner, who had left Sabine Island to go in exactly the opposite direction.

In the house at Mosquito Bay that night, suspicion smouldered and enmity was on the verge of breaking into violence; and Marius was probably the only one of the seven men who was more or less unmoved by what was happening, because he could not understand the Germans' conversation. When Ritter had agreed to the expedition to Ella Island, he had hoped for at least a month of peace while Schmidt was away. Now, suddenly and unexpectedly confronted, imprisoned by the storm in the little house with the man he believed was the author of all his problems, the man of whom he was mortally afraid, Ritter tried to defend himself by silence, by only offering the vaguest explanation of what he had been doing and why he had decided to come south.

The silence can only have added to Schmidt's suspicion. No doubt the possibility entered his mind that Ritter had been planning to desert. It was certainly one obvious explanation of his forced march to the south, and of his reticence; and Schmidt, if anyone, must have known that his own half-veiled threats of prosecution were enough to have driven his commanding officer to the most desperate of decisions. But this was only a guess. If Schmidt had made such a serious accusation, he could not have dropped it again: he could only have followed it up by arresting his commander. That was not impossible; indeed, the Nazi faction, during the winter, had often discussed it. But Schmidt had no interest in arresting him then and there at Mosquito Bay, because it would have meant abandoning the expedition to Ella Island to take Ritter under escort back to base.

Ritter told them all that now he had seen Mosquito Bay, he was satisfied and meant to drive back to Sabine Island, and as a matter of fact that was true. He had never thought of desertion. Whether Schmidt believed the statement or not, it suited him to accept it for the present.

Yet another subject of disagreement came to a head that night. When Ritter had let Peter go to Sandodden, he had not bothered to try to explain to the Nazis how he had reasoned that if Peter did run for it, he could not do any harm; he had just let them go on believing that he thought Peter would wait till the Germans came to fetch him. Now, he had to pay for this omission. On their way to Mosquito Bay, Dr. Weiss and his party, with Schmidt among them, had spent a night at Sandodden themselves, and had seen the sledge which Peter had exchanged and left there; and on their way up Loch Fyne before the storm, they had identified his tracks. So now once again the Nazis had proved to be right, to Schmidt's satisfaction, and Ritter wrong. To have given his reason now would have seemed no more than a lame excuse; and so he had to swallow Schmidt's hints that a humble hunter had made a fool of him.

It was on that night of bitter suppressed dissension that Marius first learned for certain that Weiss and the others intended an attack on Ella Island. They asked him, through Ritter as interpreter, or else Ritter asked him on his own initiative, which was the best route for them to take, the short way across the open ice, or the way back through the Badlands and then through Musk Ox Fjord. He advised them at once to go back through Musk Ox Fjord, and told them the open sea-ice at that time of year would be dangerous. Ritter passed on the advice and persuaded them to accept it; and when the weather cleared they harnessed up and set off together up the valley, leaving Ritter and Marius to prepare for their journey back to Hansa Bay.

When Marius had first encountered the Germans, he had been slow in his reaction, but a fortnight of plotting in captivity had sharpened his wits. Afterwards, he could not have said how he evolved the plan which he made at Mosquito Bay, whether he thought it all out or whether it came to him in a flash of inspiration; but certainly he knew about the loose deep snow in Musk Ox Fjord, and he knew in the split second when the Germans asked his advice that he had it in his power to thwart them. It worked: the four inexperienced drivers, who had come down through the Badlands without much trouble, found it a very different matter to go up, after a week of fresh snowfall and wind. Their sledges bogged down and the dogs floundered on their bellies in the snow and could not find a foothold. The sledges were heavily laden, with more food and equipment than more experienced travellers would have carried, and machine-guns, ammunition and hand grenades. The drivers sweated and heaved on the sledges themselves. When at last they had crossed the stretch of land, they found that

Musk Ox Fjord was worse. Indeed, it was worse than Marius could have expected. A warm wind called the Föhn, which sometimes mysteriously blows down from the ice cap, was sweeping through the funnel of the fjord. This wind can raise the temperature within an hour from 15° below freezing point to 15° above it, and it plays havoc with the ice. The Germans found slush and salt water on the ice in Musk Ox Fjord. Two days later, they were still only half-way down the fjord. They must have been angry, and because Ritter had given them the advice to go that way, they must have blamed him for their delays.

In Mosquito Bay, an hour after the others were out of sight, Ritter was baking bread in preparation for the journey back to Sabine Island. He told Marius he could go out to feed the dogs; and Marius went, and saw what he had hoped for. When they arrived, and the house had been full of Germans, Ritter had left his rifle on the sledge; and now he had forgotten to take it in. It was still in its holster on the sledge's handle bar. Marius took it and saw that it was loaded, and crept back to the window of the house and looked in. Ritter was standing with his back to him, kneading dough. Marius went to the door, with his finger on the trigger. Ritter heard him, and looked over his shoulder, and saw and understood, and made a movement towards a cupboard on his right, but his hands were covered thick in sticky dough, and he knew he was caught. Marius glanced in the direction of his movement, and saw the revolver lying on top of the cupboard. "Stand still," he said to Ritter; and he edged over to the cupboard, covering Ritter, and got the revolver too.

Ritter stood scraping the dough from his fingers. There had never been much need for conversation between those men: there was not much now. Ritter did not need to be told that the tables were turned and that he was the prisoner now, or that Marius was going to be a stricter and more efficient warder than he had been himself. All he said was, "What are you going to do?" and he probably knew the answer.

"I'm going to Ella Island," Marius told him.

28

WHEN MARIUS had gone, Ritter sat alone by the stove in the house at Mosquito Bay. All will to any action was drained out of him, all his hope was gone; and yet strangely, he felt at peace.

Marius had not wasted any time in harnessing his team, and had not given Ritter the slightest chance to fight; and when Ritter had watched him, with his eight splendid dogs and an almost empty sledge, driving down to the ice and out across the bay which he had said so convincingly was dangerous, he had not the slightest doubt he would get to Ella first and warn its garrison, or that when the German party arrived at the end of its longer slower journey, it would find an ambush waiting. What would happen? The Germans were much better armed than the Danes, and would probably fight their way out again; and Schmidt, at least, would never, never believe that Ritter had not planned to get him killed. Even Weiss and Sensse and any of the others who might have friendly feelings towards him could hardly fail to suspect him.

It was so obvious. Ritter had spoken to Marius in a language the others could not understand. Between them, they had given the advice to take the longer route. The moment the Germans had gone, Ritter to all appearances had sent Marius, by the route they had both said was impassable, to tell the enemy garrison that the German raid was coming. It would appear as high treason and attempted murder, and he would never be able to argue against the circumstantial evidence. Even the motive was there, and was sufficient. The prosecutors would point out that Schmidt was the man who had assembled all the evidence of his earlier crimes, and that he knew it. By plotting the death of Schmidt, they would suggest, he was hoping to destroy the previous evidence and return undisputed to his command and perhaps get the *Sachsen* out and arrive back in Germany to expect congratulations and promotion.

Dwelling alone on this new turn of fate, Ritter never considered the possibility that the imaginary plot might succeed and Schmidt be killed. Armed as the Germans were, it was hardly worth considering. No: Schmidt would escape the trap; and fate or luck or chance, or the will of God, had finally and absolutely delivered Ritter to his hands. He now had a case for the worst of all possible accusations, a case which he would sincerely believe himself; and when it was added to all that had gone before, the case was unanswerable.

In the long run, this extra accusation might not have made very much difference. One might as well be hung for a sheep as a lamb, and Ritter had already been convinced he was sure to be hung. But it would bring on the crisis, and put an end to the armed truce which had been maintained so precariously between himself and the Nazis. If Schmidt and he both got back to Hansa Bay alive, it would be open war; and because Ritter was unwilling to drag any of his men into the quarrel on his side, he would simply have to submit to arrest, or summary execution.

Yet he felt peaceful. He had thought himself guilty of the death of Knudsen, but he was innocent of plotting the death of Schmidt. He would never have cold-bloodedly planned the death of a personal enemy; like most other civilised people, he would not have damned his own soul for the sake of avoiding an earthly punishment. He might have reflected that if he had been the kind of man who could have planned such a thing, he would at least have found some more certain method, and not have left it to such a slender chance. But if one is accused of attempted murder, that kind of argument does not lend much weight to one's defence; and Ritter was no longer interested in his defence. He was prepared to be accused of trying to murder Schmidt, and even of callously letting Dr. Weiss and Dr. Sensse and their other two companions also run into a trap; and he was prepared to be condemned for it, and to accept his punishment as expiation for the death of Knudsen.

He felt peaceful also because there was nothing left for him to do. Events had moved out of his hands. Marius had taken the sledge and the rifle and the revolver. Perhaps if Ritter had been in mental health and if he had had some overwhelming motive to get back to Hansa Bay, he might have made plans to try to walk there. It was 130 miles away. There was no food left in the huts on the way, except perhaps at Sandodden; unarmed, he would have had to carry all his food for the journey on his back, and a sleeping-bag and everything else he needed. There was an excellent chance of meeting polar bears, especially on the last stretch towards Sabine Island. It was not so far as Poulsen had walked, with the all-important difference that he had had a rifle: but Ritter was nearly twenty years older than Poulsen. It was a journey which would have been very unlikely to succeed, whoever tried it, and for Ritter in his present condition it was quite impossible. Even the effort of imagining the details of the journey was beyond him.

There was plenty of food of limited kinds in the house at Mosquito Bay, sacks of flour and coffee and sugar which had been left there two years before when the weather station closed down. Without a sledge or a rifle, Ritter was imprisoned in the house; but he could live there on bread and coffee. He hardly wondered what would happen in the end. Perhaps, after months, he would die there, of scurvy if nothing else had killed him first. Perhaps one day the Danes would come and find him. Perhaps Schmidt and the other men, or some of them, survivors from a battle at Ella Island, would come back that way and take him with them back to the base to face his trial. Perhaps they would return to Hansa Bay and find he had not come back, and come to hunt him. But he could not concentrate his attention on such things: he could not care.

Some time after Marius had gone, Ritter stood up and noticed that the dough he had mixed was still on the table. It had risen. He stoked up the fire, and put it in the oven; and he began to tidy up the house, entirely absorbed in trivialities.

29

MARIUS HAD been sorry to abandon Ritter, but the urgent necessity of warning Ella Island entirely outweighed his compunction at leaving one man to fend for himself. Besides, to have left him at Mosquito Bay was quite a different thing from leaving him somewhere on Hochstetter Foreland. The house was well stocked, and there was a good chance his own people would pick him up again.

Marius drove like the devil. The ice was hard, his sledge was light, his dogs were in excellent health, and there were ninety miles ahead of him. He was confident that barring accidents he would get there first; but he had to get there in time for his warning to be some use, in time for the defence of the station to be organised, and that meant the sooner the better. So he drove on, urging his dogs without mercy, through the afternoon and through the night.

By then, the second half of April, there was no darkness left at all. It was only ten days or so before the midnight sun began, and there was not much more than a hint of dusk at night. But at night it was very much colder, and then the sledge ran more easily and the dogs were more energetic.

Marius went straight down the open coast to Cape Franklin, and across the mouth of Kaiser Franz Joseph Fjord to Cape Humboldt, and into the narrow entrance of Sofia Sound. Beneath the long shadows of night, with the sky still light above, the sound stretched out before him, perfectly quiet, straight and narrow between the mountains, apparently endless. There is a hunting station at Cape Humboldt, and several huts along the sound, but he only made a brief stop at Cape Humboldt, and after that he pressed on without a pause. On the evening after he left Mosquito Bay, he saw the Bastion of Ella Island a dozen miles away and cursed his dogs on towards it. They were dead beat, and so was he. An hour later, he could see the house, and hoped that somebody in it would see him. But no sledge came out to meet him: no movement, no smoke from the chimney: the shutters were closed on the windows. With a sinking heart he drew up to the house and stopped; and then he saw three circles on the door.

He went into the empty living-room. It was quite cold. When he had opened the shutters, he saw a note and a map on the table. The note was addressed to him and signed by Poulsen and dated the 19th of April, two days earlier. It said they had done what they could to search for him but had given it up, and now, in accordance with the governor's orders, they were going south to Scoresby Sound. They would hunt on the way, and leave depots of dog food in case he escaped and had to make the journey in a hurry. The map showed him the route to Scoresby Sound, which he had never travelled before, and Poulsen had marked the places where he would leave the depots.

Marius looked at the map and folded it up and put it in his pocket. So they had all gone, and his rush of ninety miles had been wasted, and he was alone with exhausted dogs, without a friend on the whole of the north-east coast: and Schmidt and his fellow-Germans, with luck, were a couple of days behind him.

30

POULSEN AND Ziebell had been as far as Cape Humboldt and up the south side of Kaiser Franz Joseph Fjord, searching for the Akre brothers and also, but without much hope, for any sign of Marius. They had not found any of the three men, but also they had not found any Germans; and that ruled out the theory that the brothers had been captured. On the coast, in normal conditions, one traveller never worries about another if he just disappears for a week or two. Everyone is expected to cope with the ordinary dangers of travelling and to stand on his own feet: otherwise, nobody would ever be free of worry. So once Poulsen had made sure that the brothers had not fallen foul of the Germans, he could leave them to look after themselves and be reasonably sure they would turn up safely. He left notes in the huts they might visit, telling them to clear out for Scoresby Sound.

When he and Ziebell got back to Ella Island, they reported by radio to Eske Brun, and were told to give up any further search and come south themselves.

They took their time on the journey, hunting and laying their depots for Marius. The journey from Ella Island to Scoresby Sound is tedious, for all the landmarks in sight are far away, and in the tremendous scale of King Oscar's Fjord the illusion is specially strong that the mountains are small and near, and that the most strenuous efforts only carry one forward at a snail's pace. The fjord is straight, a hundred miles long and fifteen miles wide; in ordinary weather the whole length of it is visible from one end to the other. On the left as one travels down it is the rampart of the 4000 foot cliffs of Traill Island, and on the right the innumerable peaks of the Stauning Alps, which rise out of the fjord to a height of 8500 feet. In the clear air, these magnificent mountains are dwarfed to half their size, and the fjord looks as if one could stroll across it in an hour; but if one tries, at the end of an hour one is still under the shelter of the shore one has left, and the other side looks as far away as ever.

From the mouth of the fjord, when at last the traveller has reached it, the outer coast can be followed all the way to Scoresby Sound; but the moving pack ice there is close in-shore, and the ice conditions vary from storm to storm; so the usual route leads up Carlsberg Fjord and then overland to the head of Hurry Inlet. The stretch of 27 miles between these fjords is the longest crossing of land on any of the customary sledge routes on the north-east coast.

Ziebell and Poulsen, taking it easy, accomplished this journey in eleven days. They arrived in the settlement on April 30th, and found it in a state of turmoil.

Scoresby Sound is a village of thirty or forty wooden houses, widely scattered around the church, the shop, the school and the house of the head of the settlement. It is self-governing, under the authority of the Greenland administration, and is run by its head man and a kind of parish council, all of whom are Eskimos. It must have a good claim to be the most isolated village in the world, and its parish council to be the most independent body of its kind; for it is quite impossible to get into the place or out of it, except of course by sledge to the uninhabited coast, for at least ten months of every year. Its nearest neighbouring village is 450 miles farther south, and its parent government in the capital, on the opposite side of Greenland, is so utterly remote from it that the most usual way to get there, in peacetime, would be to go down to Denmark and start again from there; a journey so long that if a man from Scoresby Sound had to visit the capital, he would have to wait to come home till the following year. Except when the annual ship comes in, Scoresby Sound manages its own affairs, and manages them so well that it has never had any need for such complications as policemen, or for anything more than occasional advice, which it gets through it radio, from larger less happy communities.

Nothing like the German threat from the north had ever happened before in Scoresby Sound. It is easy enough, looking back, to say that the threat was much less than it seemed, and even to laugh, though not without sympathy, at the fears of the people; but their fears were not really ill-founded, and the important fact is that it seemed at the time, to the people who lived there, that Armageddon was coming, and the most dreadful prophecies about to be fulfilled. The mere existence of nineteen Germans some hundreds of miles away had caused the most desperate apprehension, because the people knew nothing of Germans or of war or self-defence; but even to Poulsen, who did know a little about them, the threat seemed serious enough. There were nineteen Germans and upwards of eighty able-bodied Eskimos; but he knew that whatever happened, the Eskimos would not fight, they would passively suffer, as their Christian religion had taught them; they would turn the other cheek. He did not pretend to know what whims of strategy guided the Germans,

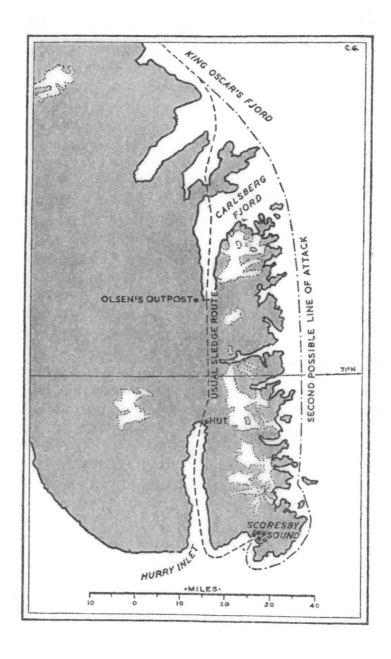

Sledge Patrol's district: southern part

but he did know it was possible they might decide that they ought to obliterate Scoresby Sound, and that if they did, they would turn the Eskimos out in the snow and burn the village down. They had done that in other places, in Russia and Poland and Norway. It was not up to people like Poulsen to guess where they would do it again. For that matter, they had done it at Eskimoness; and Scoresby Sound, like Eskimoness, was sending weather reports on its civil radio to the Americans and British.

From his solitary command, when he sledged out of Hurry Inlet, Poulsen suddenly found himself facing the perplexities of the military governor of a civil population. After the winter at Eskimoness, he felt bewildered at having to contend with a mass of people and a welter of rumour and speculation, and having to try to extract decisions out of a sea of conflicting emotions. It was like Ella Island but ten times worse, because there were ten times as many men and ten times as many opinions, besides women to be placated and children to be considered. In peaceful times, Scoresby Sound had been a kind of Paris for the men on the north-east coast, but their visits to it, which were very rare indeed, had not usually lasted very long. The kindness and hospitality of the Scoresby Sound people had been delightful but exhausting, and after the first excitement had worn off, the hunters had been used to go back to the north with a feeling they needed a rest. Now, in its state of chaotic tension, the village was more exhausting than ever before. The people were as welcoming as usual, but every single one of them wanted to ask questions and explain his own theory, and expected oracular reassuring answers. It was lucky for Poulsen, in those first few days, that Ziebell was with him there. The people knew Ziebell and he knew them, because he had been with them all the winter, and so he was able to guide Poulsen through the maze of village politics.

The place could hardly have been more difficult to defend. The only kind of defence it already possessed was a system of air-raid warnings which Ziebell had instituted, and a few shelters. Its houses extended over several miles of shore, and it had two opposite approaches, down Hurry Inlet and down the outer coast. Its people depended for their food and livelihood on hunting journeys, and hunters in the distance on their sledges could not be distinguished from attackers. Poulsen's fighting force consisted of five men with rifles: himself, Ziebell, Kurt Olsen, Peter Nielsen and Henry Rudi; and even of these, it was only the three Danes he could count on to back him wholeheartedly in a fight. Henry Rudi's position was rather equivocal. He had signed on as a civilian in the sledge patrol, but nobody had asked him if he wanted to join the Greenland Army, and nobody had reflected that after all, he was Norwegian; he had simply been told he was a corporal. It was years since he had heard anything from his own country's authorities, and Poulsen knew he had some doubt, which was more than justifiable, whether he ought to be serving in time of war in a foreign army. Henry was also the man whose arctic trust of his fellow men was most deeply a part of his character, perhaps because he had been in the arctic much longer than the others. Certainly, after Eskimoness and the news of the death of Knudsen, his trust had been shaken, but he would probably still have found it hard to aim his gun at a fellow man and fire it. Poulsen had enough of this spirit left in him to respect it; but from his present point of view, which in spite of himself was wholly military, he had to rank Henry half-way between the rest of his companions and the Eskimos, and to shut his mind to the possibility that Henry was right.

Poulsen and Ziebell and the others, escaping from the crowd into the little house which had been Ziebell's headquarters, talked over the situation till they were dizzy, and reduced it to two or three basic ideas. One blessing was that things could only go on as they were for a limited time. It was then the beginning of May. By the end of the month, the thaw would have started, and for most of June, when the fjord ice was turning to slush and the land was under flood, nobody would be able to threaten the village except by air; and what happened in July, when the seas were open, was too distant to worry about. Another hard fact was that although they had been sent back to the settlement to defend it, any active defence would have to take place outside it. If the Germans got into it, it would already be too late to defend it: a gun battle in among the houses would be certain to kill more Eskimos than Germans, and would give the Danes no chance to make use of their only kinds of superiority, a knowledge of the country and a knowledge of sledges and dogs.

So they made up their minds to sally forth to meet any enemy forces which might be on the way, and to establish an outpost as far north as they could. There were too few of them to cover both approaches, but weighing it up they decided to go up Hurry Inlet and take a chance on neglecting the outer coast. The ideal defence position, they reckoned, was right up in King Oscar's Fjord, beyond the place where the possible routes divided. If they could meet the Germans there, there was a conceivable possibility that they could harass them all down the last hundred miles of their approach, and even wear them out by guerrilla tactics.

They also decided to make one last appeal to the Americans to send over an aircraft and drop them a machine-gun. One machine-gun would have made all the difference in the world. They would have put all their savings together and bought one if they could.

Poulsen made up his mind to lead the somewhat forlorn expedition himself, and to take Ziebell and Kurt Olsen with him, leaving Henry Rudi and Peter Nielsen to encourage the Scoresby Sound people and help them to build themselves new shelters. The portable transmitter had been brought from Ella Island, and he intended to take it with him to keep communication between the outpost and the settlement. Two of the Eskimo drivers in the sledge patrol, Aparte and Christian, volunteered to come with him, and he said he would be glad to have them and that they could go back whenever they thought they had come far enough. Everything was ready; but before they could start, the weather broke and made travel impossible.

On the whole, the storm was welcome. It did nothing to soothe the fears of the Eskimos. If the threat had alarmed them in fine weather, when one could see right up Hurry Inlet and a good distance along the coast, it was even more alarming to look out and see nothing but swirling snow and to imagine the Germans might be lurking any-where, perhaps only fifty yards away. During the storm, a dozen new rumours a day were brought to Poulsen, and each of them had to be disproved. Sledges were sighted, gunfire and aircraft were reported. The storm was a nervous strain; but from a reasonable point of view, it was a respite. Unless one allowed oneself to be infected with the belief that Germans were superhuman, one knew they simply could not approach in such weather; and each day of impassable storm was one day nearer to the finally impassable thaw.

The weather began to clear on the 9th of May, and on the 10th Poulsen was on the way up Hurry Inlet, with his four sledges close behind him. He and his men were thankful to be out in the wilder-ness again, and to be going to look for trouble instead of waiting for trouble to come to them; Scoresby Sound had given them a kind of claustrophobia. At the head of the inlet, there is a hut; and in accordance with the prudent tactics which they had learned at such expense, they stopped a couple of miles away and looked at it through glasses: and there were sledges and dogs outside it.

These could only be sledges from the north, and so they sur-rounded the hut at a distance and approached it cautiously; but there was no sign of life from inside, and Poulsen, half expecting some subtle trap, crept right up to the house, trigger conscious, before the dogs woke up and howled at him in furious alarm. Then the door opened and two sleepy but apprehensive men peered out:

the two missing brothers from Ella Island, who had got there the night before on their journey south.

Both parties to this unexpected meeting felt they had been made to look a little foolish, and conversation was rather stilted; but the brothers had one important piece of news. After they had found Poulsen's notes in the huts round Sofia Sound, they had come south without going back to the house at Ella Island. In fact, they had passed the island in a fog and had not seen the house at all; but they had crossed a lot of fresh sledge tracks which led towards it. Working it out, there was only one answer: the tracks were German. Up till then, Poulsen had never had any definite news of Germans south of Eskimoness, and it had been a mere surmise that they might be roaming about the coast. Now he knew they had got as far as Ella. This news, and the acquisition of two more rifles, made Poulsen change his plans. He sent Ziebell and Olsen on, with the portable transmitter, two sledges and a tent, to establish an outpost somewhere in Carlsberg Fjord; and he went back with the two newcomers to report to Eske Brun and to try to organise a second line of defence.

Two days later, things came to a crisis. Kurt Olsen and Ziebell had got to Carlsberg Fjord, and had been in communication with Scoresby Sound radio. They had pitched the tent at a place where they had a good view to the northward, but Kurt reported the weather was getting foggy. Then suddenly, his transmitter went off the air.

Poulsen waited for news from the settlement radio station with some anxiety, while they tried to make contact again. It was likely enough that Kurt's sudden silence meant nothing worse than a fault in the portable transmitter: but it might have meant anything from that to a shot from a German sniper or a burst of machine-gun fire through the walls of the solitary tent.

While he waited, a young Eskimo hunter came in. He was excited, and his story was confused. He had been hunting in Hurry Inlet.

There was another party of men in the hut at the head of it. He had seen two men, and spoken to one of them, who said his name was Marius Jensen. There were nineteen dogs, and four pairs of skis and one sledge. He had driven home quickly.

The hunter had a companion with him, the assistant priest of the settlement. Poulsen sent for him post-haste. He added to the story. One of the men was in uniform and had a revolver in his belt. The one called Jensen had said something about musk-ox hunting and fresh sledge tracks up in Carlsberg Fjord, but he had not been able to understand him very well. There were at least nineteen dogs, he thought there were more, but there was only one sledge.

The significance of nineteen dogs and one sledge was the crux of the story. Twelve dogs was the absolute maximum which would be used with one sledge, and eight or ten was more usual. Therefore from seven to eleven spare dogs had been seen. Other sledges must have been away somewhere, each with only a part of its team. Seven spare dogs meant at least two more sledges. From what had been said, it seemed likely they were hunting, or following the fresh tracks they had seen, perhaps following them back to the outpost in Carlsberg Fjord. The time coincided with the silence of the radio.

The report suggested a force at the very least of five or six men. There was only one conclusion: that the Germans who had been at Ella Island and captured it without a fight were looking for further conquests and aiming at Scoresby Sound. It might or might not be true that one of the party was Marius. They might have used his name as some kind of bluff, or they might have forced him to come with them as a sledge driver and guide.

The sledge patrol went out to meet the enemy: Poulsen, Peter, Henry and the two Akres. As they drove westwards out of Scoresby Sound, Poulsen looked back beyond the little houses, and there, rolling in from the open sea, he saw the fog: the fog which had blinded his outpost and let the intruders past. White and dense, it floated

inexorably on, blotting out the radio station and then the more distant houses, moving faster than the sledges, rapidly catching them up;
and Poulsen saw looming in it his ultimate defeat, for his last hope
had been to ambush the German forces at the mouth of Hurry Inlet,
but now, if the fog came in and filled the inlet, he would hardly have
the slightest chance of seeing them. There was a moment then when
everything seemed lost.

Often in war men sally forth to meet tremendous odds and then
by some sudden twist of fortune find that the summoning of their
courage has been wasted. It is a curious fact that they are often angry
when they find they are not called upon to die. This happened to
Poulsen. Sledges came hurrying out to intercept him, from the last
houses in the settlement. Their Eskimo drivers called him to come
in. Two strangers had arrived. They had only eight dogs. The hunter's
and the priest's imaginations had added eleven more. The man called
Jensen, the Eskimos said, was little but he must be very strong. He
must have been beating the tall man, because he was crying. Poulsen
followed them in, quite unable to imagine what he would find.

There was Marius with his sledge, and another man, a stranger.

"Marius!" Poulsen said. "Who's that?"

"My prisoner," Marius said. They were men of few words. The tall
man had been tearing the medals and distinctions off his uniform,
and now he was sitting with his face buried in his hands.

31

IT TOOK Poulsen a very long time to gather the story of Marius's escape, piecing it together like a jigsaw puzzle from the occasional scraps of laconic information which he managed to wring out of him. But even the few facts which Marius could bring himself to put into words were enough to suggest he had made a rather remarkable journey; for he had left Sabine Island on April 5th, and got to Scoresby Sound on May 13th, and he had travelled on every day of those five and a half weeks, and covered a distance of round about 800 miles, mostly with Ritter, but partly alone.

At the end of his dash to Ella Island, when he had found that all the others had gone south, there was one obvious thing for him to do, and that was to follow them and waste no time about it. Weiss and his squad were on the way, a day or two behind him, with a plentiful supply of lethal weapons, and it was easy enough to guess that if they turned up and caught him there, they would be very angry men.

Poulsen and Ziebell, a day or two ahead of him, had told him in their note they were travelling slowly to hunt on his behalf. His dogs were tired, but he could have caught up with the others and travelled in safety and comfort to Scoresby Sound. It was the obvious thing to do, and he did not do it: he went back to Mosquito Bay to see what had happened to Ritter.

When Poulsen asked Marius why, he replied with an amiable grin: "Because I knew you'd ask such a hell of a lot of questions. I thought I'd better get Ritter to answer them." And for years afterwards, there the matter rested.

But Marius was not simply being obstinate: the fact was that he hardly knew why he had done it himself. It was a crazily dangerous thing to have done. But it had been an impulse, and Marius was not the sort of man who is used to analysing his own motives for impulsive actions. Left to himself, he would never have thought any more about it; but Poulsen's probing had forced him to delve in his own mind, and he had glimpsed the truth and covered it up again: for the truth was that he had done it out of pure and simple kindness. People are often ashamed to say that charity had been their motive, either because they are afraid of boasting or because they are afraid of being laughed at. Back among his matter-of-fact colleagues at Scoresby Sound, Marius was afraid of both; and he had an added peculiar difficulty: for in wartime it is hard to say in so many words that one likes one's enemies' commander.

Yet that was the simple explanation of a gallant gesture. At Ella Island, when Marius had had to make up his mind so quickly, he had felt ashamed to have stolen Ritter's rifle and left him all alone at Mosquito Bay. At the time, he had done it with a clear conscience, because of the need to warn the sledge patrol at Ella; but as soon as he had found there was nobody there to warn, he had felt remorseful. By then, he had already travelled a long way with Ritter, man to man. Ritter had treated him fairly and decently. They had been through a lot together; and now, by all arctic standards, he had played him a dirty trick. Besides, he had an oddly protective feeling for the man who had been his captor. He had sometimes seemed to be a vague and helpless person. Marius was afraid he might not know how to look after himself now that he was alone; he might die at Mosquito Bay. He thought he would be better off as a prisoner at Scoresby Sound. He did not stop to think much about the risk to himself, which was tremendous; he just set off to take help to a man, another traveller, who might be in difficulties.

He drove back the ninety miles along Sofia Sound and across the sea-ice, not so fast as he had come, but fast enough; and five days after he had left Mosquito Bay he was back there again.

By that time, Marius was a shrewd campaigner, and he had no intention of being captured again if he could help it; so he circled round the house, two miles away, until he had accounted for each track that led into it or out: three sledge tracks in from the Badlands Valley and two out, and his own outgoing track across the bay. There were no others, and the chimney was smoking; so Ritter was still there, and still alive, and still alone. He drove up to the house, and left his dogs in harness.

Ritter, seeing the sledge approaching, had not really been surprised to recognise Marius. He was almost beyond surprise. In the solitude of the house, his mind had faded into a kind of half-deliberate day-dream which excluded all thoughts of war. He had been sleeping a lot, and when he was awake, or half awake, he had only been thinking of his family and of peaceful arctic things: and so he was glad to see Marius back so soon, forgetting that it was strange that a prisoner who had escaped should come back to the place he had escaped from, and that he had never expected to see him back at all.

But Marius roused him. He had come back to help, but there was only one kind of help he could give, and it had to be given quickly. As he came in at the door, he just said: "Get your clothes on. We're going south." Within a few minutes, they were away again; but before they went, Marius asked Ritter to promise not to give him any trouble, and Ritter, still bewildered, said he would. So began the most curious journey recorded in the arctic; for Marius had to escort the enemy commander alone for 290 miles, through territory which the enemy, if anyone, controlled. It took him fifteen days.

Could Ritter have escaped? This question was asked, long after it was all over, by the Germans and Danes alike. The literal answer must be that he could. Marius took all the precautions he could think of to prevent it, because he could not be certain whether to treat Ritter as an arctic comrade or an enemy; but of course there were moments, especially in the first few days and nights, when Ritter could have taken Marius unawares and got the rifle back. Those chances could not be avoided. Ritter could have escaped by killing Marius, or leaving him in a situation in which he was likely to die; just as Marius could have escaped, up in the distant north, by killing Ritter. But Marius had tied his prisoner with a subtler bond; for the point was that there was never a single moment when Ritter could have escaped without killing Marius: and of course, though Marius himself could not be sure of this, no earthly compulsion, by then, could have made Ritter commit such a crime. He would not have killed any man, and even more certainly, perhaps, he would not have killed Marius; because it was Marius who had been his guide on the journey when he had first felt freedom again, and because now, soon after they left Mosquito Bay, he understood that Marius had risked his own life and his own freedom to come back and look after him; so that Marius had shown him at last that the old arctic principles of conduct were still alive. It was Marius's achievement not that he cowed his prisoner into going quietly, but that he showed him, just by being himself, an example which made his prisoner unable to raise a hand against him.

No doubt by then Ritter's will to escape had weakened too. He was a very tired man: initiative had been beaten out of him by the Nazis in his own command. He was feeling very old. If he had escaped, his command would have been taken away from him by the Nazis, and by all common sense that put an end to his military duty to escape. If Marius had given him a chance, he would still have felt a duty to go back and face his punishment: but that could never have been an incentive to commit another murder.

So they travelled in a kind of unspoken truce. Two men with a sledge can only travel in equal positions, one on each side of the sledge. The sledge goes too fast, except in soft snow, for a man on skis to follow; he can only keep up by holding on to the sledge with one hand. So Ritter skied on the left of the sledge and Marius on the right, each with a hand on the raised bar at the back of the sledge. Marius had the revolver in his belt, and his shooting hand was free except when he was using the dog whip or a ski stick. The rifle was in its holster, close to him in its usual position on the right-hand side of the sledge. It was mostly when they stopped to rest and eat, or to manhandle the sledge or sort out the traces of the dogs, or to change over from a fan to a tandem trace, that Ritter could have hit Marius from behind, or snatched the rifle.

At nights, when they stopped at huts, they ate together, and then Marius left Ritter to sleep in the hut and pitched the tent some distance away and slept there with the dogs picketed round him. When there was no hut, Ritter slept in the tent, and Marius went away with the dogs and slept on the sledge in the open. Again, these precautions were better than nothing, but they did not give Marius any real security. If Ritter had come out and tried to creep up on him, the dogs might have woken up and howled and given Marius a warning; but on the other hand, they knew Ritter nearly as well by then as they knew their own master, and they might have wagged their tails and gone to sleep again.

In the first part of the journey, Marius had to hunt to feed Ritter and himself and the dogs. Then he left Ritter in a hut and went out with the dogs. Sometimes, if it was musk-ox, he picketed the dogs out of Ritter's immediate reach, and followed his quarry into the hills on foot. Perhaps these were the safest times of all. Ritter could have got up and walked away, but there was nowhere for him to walk to, and Marius could easily have trailed him with the sledge and caught him up.

But the danger for Marius all through the first few days was not from Ritter at all; it was from Schmidt. By the time Marius got back to Mosquito Bay, Schmidt and the other four men might just about be expected to have got to Ella Island. There was absolutely no way of guessing how long they would stay there when they found the place deserted. There was no knowing whether they had the skill to pick out his tracks among all the others round the station, and to observe that they were only a day or two old and came and went through Sofia Sound. Above all, Marius could not tell whether the Germans would go back by the way they had come, or try the short cut through Sofia Sound themselves. So for day after day, he had to expect to meet them face to face.

Of course he would have gone another way if he could, and kept out of Sofia Sound; but for all the spaciousness of the north-east coast, there is very little choice of different sledge routes. The only other way south from Mosquito Bay was right down the outer coast of Traill Island. He had never been down there, or heard of anybody who had been there so late in the year, and he thought it was even more risky. There might be no hunting, and they might have got stuck by finding broken ice right in to the foot of the sea cliffs and have had to come all the way back, or even have been cut off by the approach of the thaw and slowly starved; or on the pack ice, they might have drifted out to sea. He reckoned it was better to run the gantlet past the cliffs of Ella.

But it was very uncomfortable to enter the mouth of Sofia Sound again. The sound is narrow, three or four miles from shore to shore. There was no darkness at all. The weather stayed fine and clear. If the

two German sledges were coming up the sound in the opposite direction, there was not the slightest chance of getting past them: even if
the drivers were not keeping a lookout, the teams of dogs would scent
each other. So ominous did the sound appear, its thirty bare straight
miles stretching on the Ella Island at the far end, that Marius turned
back once and tried to take his sledge across Geographical Society
Island by a valley which seemed to lead right through the mountains;
but that way of escape was blocked by enormous drifts of snow which
was getting wet and heavy. He was forced back to the ice; so he rested
his dogs, and prepared to make a dash through the zone of danger.

For Marius, those thirty miles down the sound, and the next
twenty or so past the island itself, had something of the breath-
less suspense of hunting; but Ritter's feelings can only be imagined.
Hour after hour, Marius called on his dogs and urged them forward,
watching the ice horizon far ahead for a glimpse of the two black
specks of the other sledges. Ritter, tiring more quickly, grimly held
on to the sledge bar. The farther they went, the nearer they came
to the climax; for the end of Sofia Sound is only five miles from
the point of Ella Island, and eleven miles from the station, where
Schmidt and the others, at that very moment, were certainly lurking; and at that distance a sentry on the hills could not have failed
to see the moving sledge.

They came to the end, and turned south, and raced past the foot
of the mountains and across the mouth of Vega Sound and into the
shadow of the vast cliffs of Traill Island and the sanctuary of King
Oscar's Fjord. For three hours, they were plainly in sight from the
island, but nothing stirred, no sledge put out from it, no warning
shot was fired. At last with the island ten miles behind him and the
empty ice between, Marius could stop and rest; because after that, if
the Germans did come out to catch him, the chase would be a stern
one, and he would have backed his eight dogs against any team the
Germans might have mustered.

After the island was passed, every mile they travelled made them safer, and every mile made the idea that Ritter might escape seem more remote. Somewhere down King Oscar's Fjord they reached a point where both of them knew it was finally out of the question, because even if Ritter had murdered Marius he would not have had the strength or ability to drive the dog team back to the north again. One night, in one of the huts down there, Ritter said: "Well, the war's finished now for me." After that, they were not a prisoner and an escort any more; they were just two travellers. They shared the huts, or slept in the tent together. Sometimes, when Marius was tired, Ritter took the rifle and did the hunting. All that either of them wanted was to get to Scoresby Sound and get the journey over.

Not very much of this story was told in Scoresby Sound when they arrived, and none of its more obscure considerations came to light. A bare factual report of what Marius had done was transmitted to Eske Brun, and eventually travelled far and wide to the British and American High Commands. Somewhere, somebody added to it a strictly military motive for Marius's gallant action; for it was not inconceivable to a military mind that he had gone back in the role of a good soldier to Mosquito Bay, and taken Ritter captive simply for the sake of the military advantage it would bring. If Marius had been a soldier at all, he might have thought of that reason himself. Anyhow, he was promoted sergeant in the Greenland Army and awarded the British Empire Medal and the United States Legion of Merit. No medals are awarded for simple human kindness; but still most people think it a nobler motive, and not only in the arctic.

32

TO HAVE Ritter as a prisoner in the village did nothing at all to quieten the anxieties of the people of Scoresby Sound. If anything, it only upset them more. Rumours, which up till then had had nothing more than imaginary sledges to feed upon, attached themselves to Ritter, as if he had been a wild man who might run amok. Poulsen was woken up in the middle of the night to be told that Ritter had been seen with a dagger in his boot, and again to be told a revolver was hidden in the loft of the room where the prisoner was quartered. Sledge rumours flourished too, and one evening when unidentified sledges were sighted in the fjord and the aircraft spotter, at the same moment, happened to sound the air-raid warning, the rumour of approaching forces spread so fast that the daughter of the head of the settlement carried out her last-ditch duty of burning all the spare codes which belonged to the radio station.

Ritter and Poulsen, as was only to be expected, treated each other at first with reserve and suspicion. The Danish prisoners had been looked after well enough in Sabine Island, and Poulsen made things as comfortable as he could for Ritter in return. But Ritter was reticent, and refused to give Poulsen any military information. Poulsen imagined that a German officer's idea of duty might make him try to do some damage in Scoresby Sound, and especially perhaps to sabotage the radio station; so he kept him strictly under guard. It was a nuisance. The capture of Ritter, so far as he could tell, had not ended the chances of attack. On the contrary, Marius had confirmed the news that four Germans had been at Ella, and had been able to say exactly what arms they had; and it was not beyond belief that they now had an extra reason for coming to Scoresby Sound: to rescue their commander. For the first time, the whole of the sledge patrol was gathered together, except the one dead man; but that only meant eight rifles, and guarding the prisoner day and night took two of them. Six rifles was none too many to defend the place against four men with machine-guns and hand grenades.

But still, Marius's successful coup had put new spirit into all the sledge patrol. Their blood was up. They had never liked the retreat from Ella Island, and now it seemed a feeble policy to sit in Scoresby Sound and wait for the thaw. Once the thaw began, they would not be able to get out, any more than the Germans could get in, and they would have to wait till the seas were open and a ship from the outside came in, to take them ignominiously back to their patrol grounds. They began to talk about advancing instead of retreating, and going to see what had happened at Ella Island. The idea was put up to the government, and Eske Brun, never a man for retreat, agreed at once.

By then there was not much time to waste. It was past the middle of May, and they could not depend on much more than a fortnight of sledging. The journey to Ella would have to be a careful reconnaissance and it would take at least ten days. Therefore, it would have to be a journey without a retreat; for if they got to the station and found the Germans in possession and failed to turn them out, it would probably be too late to get back to Scoresby Sound: the ice would have melted behind them. But that would not matter unless somebody got wounded. They did not want to come back. They were prepared to wait in camp, if that was necessary, all through the thaw, anywhere in the mountains in the Ella district; and rather than come south again, if all went well and they could get the motor boat which belonged to the Ella station, they would go farther north when the fjords were clear of ice.

This week after Ritter and Marius came in had been, in fact, a turning point. Hitherto, Poulsen had not seen the faintest gleam of success since the very early days when he had triumphantly reported the German base and waited hour by hour to hear that the Americans had destroyed it. But now his campaign began to have a pattern which was strangely like a lesson in a military text-book. It may have been only due to common sense, and not to training in a staff college, but there it was: the tactical withdrawal which allowed the enemy to exhaust himself in useless territorial advances, and then the counter stroke. It only remained to be seen if the counter stroke would work.

Poulsen had to divide his force again. Now that Scoresby Sound instead of Eskimoness had become the patrol's headquarters, he supposed he ought to stay there, and after a lot of discussion, Ziebell, Kurt Olsen and Marius were chosen for the Ella expedition. Exactly a week after Marius had come in at the end of his marathon journey, he started again for the north with these two new companions. The sledge patrol had taken the initiative at last.

It was only a few days after they had gone that Poulsen received the very first sign that anyone in the outside world, except Eske Brun, was interested in his private war. A signal came to warn him to expect a friendly aircraft, and soon afterwards an enormous American bomber zoomed over Scoresby Sound and threw out a container attached to a parachute. Astonished and fascinated, everyone in the village watched the thing float down, and when it landed safely on the ice they rushed out to surround it at a distance. Poulsen unpacked it, and found at last four beautiful machine-guns. At once he sent out a signal to the Ella expedition to tell them to wait where they were, and he got two Eskimo volunteers with sledges and loaded them up with a gun and a stock of ammunition and told them to drive full speed to catch up with Ziebell and give him this invaluable prize. There was no instruction book, but he thought Ziebell would figure out how to work it.

Four days later, the Eskimo sledges were back, still carrying the machine-gun. North of the head of Hurry Inlet, the rivers were running. The thaw had begun and the sledge route was impassable. Scoresby Sound was cut off from the rest of the coast. The gun had arrived when it was just too late to matter.

33

POULSEN, SITTING impotently now in Scoresby Sound, with nothing more exciting to do than keep an eye on Ritter and try to catch up with the sledge patrol's accounts, watched the progress of the Ella expedition through their radio reports. Now that he had the machine-guns, he was even more aware of how poorly his advance party was armed, and he was relieved to hear, on the 2nd of June, that they had got to Ella and found the house still there and reoccupied it without any opposition. For a long time, he heard no more than that. They had always assumed that whatever else the Germans did at Ella, they would certainly destroy the radio transmitter, so Kurt Olsen had taken the emergency transmitter with him. But the sledges had been loaded up with camping gear for a whole summer, and they had had to cut down on radio batteries and agree only to exchange essential signals. So it was not till later in the year that Poulsen heard the comic and yet faintly sinister details of the sledge patrol's return to Ella Island.

Ziebell and Marius and Kurt Olsen, ten days out from Scoresby Sound, had made a wary approach towards the island. There was a large iceberg which had been frozen in all winter a couple of miles off the station, and they kept in the lee of it. When they got to it without seeing new tracks or raising an alarm, they hid their dogs behind it, and peering round the edge of it, observed the house through glasses. It looked exactly the same as ever. The shutters were closed, and there was no smoke and no sign of life. After they had watched it for long enough, Ziebell as the officer told Kurt and Marius, the two sergeants, to stay there and cover him while he advanced a little nearer. He roused up his dogs and drove out from behind the iceberg and steered them towards the house.

As soon as the dogs saw the house ahead of them, they took charge and began to gallop gaily towards it. Half-way there, Ziebell saw something he had not noticed from the iceberg: outside the house, there were over a dozen rifles standing in a row, piled in threes in orderly parade-ground fashion. And then he saw something else: in the shadow of the doorway a man in uniform was standing stock still and staring out to sea.

Somewhat frantically, he tried to turn his dogs and get away again, but they took no notice of his shouts or his whip and bounded straight on towards the house.

Still nothing happened. The house was silent, the man stood like a statue. The dogs swept right up to the door and sat down there, panting, and then Ziebell, with his finger on the trigger of his rifle, saw that it was a statue: at least, it was a dummy stuffed with straw. He looked at the piles of rifles. They were an old Danish pattern which had been obsolete for years and had been left in the loft at Ella because nobody had any ammunition for them.

He signaled to the others to come up, and then, having heard of booby traps, he pushed the door open with the butt of his rifle and waited for the bang. Nothing but a cold dank air came out of the living-room. He went in. The eight-day clock was ticking. On the stove was a pot of stew which was beginning to go mouldy. Looking round, he noticed something stranger. The American pin-up girls who had graced the walls for years had disappeared, and in their places were two less alluring photographs, one of Hitler and one of Mussolini. Below the one of Hitler, someone had written the revealing words: WE ARE THE BEST SOLDIERS IN THE WORLD.

It hardly seemed worth while to use up batteries to send these tidings to Poulsen, peculiar though they were; but the whole affair provided a useful subject for argument all through the summer. A rational explanation was invented for the dummy and the rifles: they might have been put there, with no intention of being ridiculous, in case a reconnaissance aircraft was sent to photograph the station. But opinion was divided. One school of thought maintained that Nazis at last had shown a sense of humour, and another that they had shown less than no sense of humour at all.

More important, though less amusing, were the other things the Germans had done at Ella. The radio transmitter and its batteries and generator and the lighting installation had all been deliberately damaged, and so had the motor boat engine; a large hole had been blown in the boat by a hand-grenade. The wooden aerial masts, ten inches thick, had been felled, cut through by machine-gun fire. The supplies of food in the station were rather depleted, as if they had fed several men for quite a time, but what was left was in good condition. A depot on the neighbouring island called Maria had been destroyed, but bears and foxes might have had something to do with that. Other depots hidden in the hills had not been touched; there was no sign that they had even been discovered.

Altogether, the damage was much less than anyone had expected. There was nothing malicious about it. It had all the appearance of a delaying action, rather than an attempt to put the station out of action altogether. Even the motors which were damaged had not been thoroughly destroyed: nobody had taken a hammer to their castings. A few days' work was enough to get the lighting motor going again, and the motor boat engine was also repaired on the spot. The hole in the boat was more difficult, but only because there were no materials at the station for shipwright's work.

Of course, there were two interpretations to be put on the Germans' half-hearted sabotage. One was that they were only interested in stopping broadcasts from Ella till the summer was well advanced, and had refrained from doing any more damage than they needed, either out of generosity, or else perhaps, to take the lowest view, because they all expected to be captured in the end and did not want to annoy the Danes too much. The other possibility was that they were not very far away and intended to come back. The latter idea was supported by the mystery of the ticking clock, for the Danes, of course, took this as conclusive evidence that the Germans had been at Ella less than a week before. As a matter of fact, it was nearly a month since the German party had done the damage and gone away, and one can only suppose that the banging of doors or footsteps on the floors had started the clock again.

So Ziebell and Kurt and Marius settled in, but kept a cautious lookout. For the present at least, the Germans had disappeared. The rivers had started to roar again, avalanches were falling in the mountains, and the ice on the fjord was getting wet and dark. Very soon, wherever the Germans had gone, they would have to stay there, and Ella Island, surrounded by miles of slush, would be safe from invasion either by ice or sea. In the meantime, the sledge patrol had got one of its stations back, and the new pair of portraits, in their turn, were torn down from the living-room walls.

34

SCORESBY SOUND was also safe, unless it was raided by air. Henry Rudi and the Akre brothers turned into air-raid wardens. The sledge patrol Eskimos started their summer jobs of mending sledges and harnesses and skis, and hunting to feed the dogs. Some Eskimo women were taken on the strength, to mend tents and winter clothes and make new ones for the next year's sledging. Peter Nielsen guarded Ritter, relieved by Poulsen when he could get away from the office work which had piled up for months.

It would have been fitting if Ritter and Poulsen, in the weeks they spent together in Scoresby Sound, had discovered in conversation that they had never wanted to fight against each other. They both suspected it, but neither of them put it into words. Meeting now, face to face, both of them wondered what would have happened that night at Eskimoness when they shouted to each other across the ice, if Ritter had kept his finger off the trigger and accepted Poulsen's offer to let one man come across the shore unarmed. In the middle of those arctic wastes, could two men who had so much in common have found a common-sense agreement, or was each of them, even there, too strongly bound by the ties of duty to his own side in the far-away battle in Europe?

In Scoresby Sound, that night and the events which followed it were too recent for open and calm discussion, and it was not till later years that either of these men could come to understand the other and appreciate his qualities. Poulsen, still weighed down at that time by all his responsibilities, could only think of Ritter's presence as yet another worry. Ritter had told him a little about the troubles he had had with the Nazis in his unit, and Poulsen believed it was true that Ritter had never been a Nazi himself; but still, he was a German officer, and Poulsen was never sure what a captive German officer might do. Perhaps Henry Rudi and Peter Nielsen got to know Ritter better, because they had less responsibility. Rudi, a shrewd judge of human beings as well as of bears, remarked quite early in Ritter's imprisonment that the man was a gentleman, using the English word with all its original honourable meaning; and he said in his forthright way that even if Ritter did try to escape, it would be wrong to try to shoot him. Peter, on the other hand, who had most of the hard work of guarding the prisoner, was quite willing to tell him he would shoot him if he gave him any trouble. He probably meant it, but he probably knew that Ritter would never do anything of the kind; for although he always wore a revolver in his belt, Peter also, to his own surprise, had begun to feel a profound admiration for Ritter. Marius, Henry, Peter: perhaps none of them quite knew why they unwillingly liked their enemy, but perhaps it is fair to guess that what they had seen in Ritter, and what they admired, was the probity which made his German uniform seem insignificant.

As for Ritter himself, after all the spiritual distress that he had suffered, his conscience was calm and his fears were ended now.

Perhaps he was glad he had been captured, though perhaps in those early days, before the confusion in his mind had quite been resolved by the passage of time, he could hardly have seen the fact which he recognised later: that Marius's uncompromising firmness on their journey had been the solution to all his problems. But solved they were. Looking back on his record as an officer, he would have admitted he had treated Marius as his prisoner too leniently, and run a risk, through lack of forethought, of being taken prisoner himself. Certainly he had been careless and foolish to leave his rifle on the sledge at Mosquito Bay. But if that could be forgiven, he felt he had done his duty to the German Navy as best he could. He had seen his men through to the spring. Nobody had ever expected the base would last all through the summer and still be there when the following winter came; and he himself, ever since the base had been detected, had assumed he would never be able to get the *Sachsen* out, and that all his men would be captured in the end. As for the Gestapo, they might judge him and condemn him for his offences against the Party; but he believed that the Navy, in his absence as a prisoner of war, would look after his wife and daughter and defend them against Gestapo revenge. Above all, he felt supremely thankful that the war was over for him, as he had said with such feeling to Marius: because for him that simply meant that never again could the power of military law or party politics be used to coerce him towards acts which seemed to him to defy the will of God.

His imprisonment in Scoresby Sound gave point to these reflections. He had never been in an Eskimo settlement before, and he would have been delighted to join in its daily life, which was so essentially arctic; but of course that was denied him. He could watch the children playing or going to school, or the Eskimos dressed in their Sunday best on their way to church; but to watch them could only make him more aware that he was the only man in the whole community who did not have the trust of every other, the only outlaw. It was he as the representative of Germany who had disrupted the orderly existence of the Eskimos and brought fear into Scoresby Sound for the very first time in its history; an achievement, he thought, of which Germany had no reason to be proud.

Yet however much he would have liked to talk on friendly terms with the Eskimos and Danes, he could not make a show of his feelings. It was not a matter of pride, or of being afraid to be rebuffed: it was a matter of humility. He had given them plenty of reason to mistrust him, and for what he had done he had to be willing to pay the price of ostracism. It was also in his own interest, as it happened, to behave consistently and correctly as a prisoner of war. Perhaps nobody would ever have heard of anything which was not within the code of an officer who was a prisoner, and if by some unforeseeable chain of rumours news of it had got to Germany, the Navy itself, as well as the Party, might have begun to doubt his loyalty, and felt less concerned to defy the Party by taking care of his wife. His own instinct and his interest coincided; and so, in Scoresby Sound, he retired into his own thoughts and made no friendly overtures.

In spite of his reticence, or perhaps because of it, the community of Scoresby Sound would soon have accepted Ritter and absorbed him. There was something in his character which, without any conscious intention, had already won over his guards; and Eskimos are too happy to harbour grudges. In time, everyone would have forgotten he had been an enemy; thins like that are easily forgotten in the arctic. But of course that could not have been allowed to happen. After a few weeks, when the sound had thawed, a seaplane came in and took him away to a prison camp in America.

But just before it came, there was an incident which was the first sign of forgiveness. There had been a rifle accident, and an Eskimo child had got a bullet in her leg. Somebody had heard that Ritter was clever as a doctor, and the Eskimos asked the Danes to let him come and help them. He went with his guard. It was almost his last act in Greenland, and perhaps it is appropriate as a final impression of this strangely attractive man. Perhaps in the Eskimo house a true glimpse of Ritter may be had, trying to soothe the pain of a child he had never seen before and would never see again, wholly absorbed in the gentle delicate operation on the wound.

35

THE END was coming quickly, not only because the thaw was impris-
oning everyone, each in his little corner of the coast, but also because
in Europe and America vast forces were stirring at last to intervene.

It is too late, fourteen years after these events took place, to delve
into the secret records of such an enormous organisation as the
United States Air Force with any hope of finding a definite answer to
the question which puzzled Poulsen: the question why nothing happened for over two months after he reported the German landing at
Hansa Bay. But of course one can guess at the answer, and one obvious guess is that although it seemed important enough to Poulsen,
the American Air Force had plenty of more important things to do.
They knew German forecasts were still going out from Sabine Island;
but after all, the summer was approaching, and weather forecasting
on the north Atlantic convoy routes was probably less decisive in summer than in winter. In summer, as the midnight sun began, the arctic

convoys to Russia had to stop, and in general the important activities of war, for which darkness was still convenient, tended to drift away towards the south. Perhaps, from the point of view of global strategy, once the winter was over, the German base at Sabine Island did not matter very much, provided it was demolished before the following autumn. In war, almost all operations are urgent and cannot wait; but the attack on Sabine Island could.

Perhaps in the end even Poulsen was not altogether sorry there had been such a long delay. Things had not worked out too badly after all, and he might have regretted it if the great impersonal forces of mechanised war had invaded the coast too soon and made his job too easy.

The bombing of Sabine Island was a difficult undertaking. It needed Liberators and Flying Fortresses fitted with long-range tanks, and it also needed aircrews trained in arctic flying. The Americans' leading expert for a raid of that kind was the veteran Norwegian pilot, Bernt Balchen, who was a colonel then in the United States Air Force. He had flown Admiral Byrd on his south polar expeditions, and had been a pioneer of flying in the arctic, and he knew more about polar flying than anyone else in the world at that time; and indeed he still does. In that spring, he was on the south-west coast of Greenland in charge of American airfields, but for several months he had been preoccupied with rescuing the crew of a bomber which had crashed on the Greenland ice-cap; and that may perhaps have been an added reason why Sabine Island was left to itself so long. Anyhow, in May, the rescue was completed, and Bernt Balchen flew to Iceland to prepare a final retribution fort the base in Hansa Bay.

But before the bombers went to Hansa Bay, they made a separate expedition to attack Eskimoness. This puzzled the sledge patrol even more when they came to hear of it. No doubt the intention was to prevent the Germans from using the place as a refuge, but something must have gone wrong with liaison somewhere, because anyone on the coast itself could have said that there was nothing left at Eskimoness to bomb. Peter Nielsen and Marius Jensen had both seen the empty space where once the house had stood. However, the bombs went down, and scattered its ashes even farther, and on May 29th, unknown to Poulsen, the heavy force of bombers reached Hansa Bay.

For three hours, the arctic quiet was shattered by engines and bombs and gunfire as plane after plane roared over the Sabine hills. The Germans fought back. But when it was all over, none of the aircraft had been damaged and surprisingly little damage had been done on the ground. A hut had been set on fire by incendiary bullets and the meteorological gear was put out of action; but according to German reports the *Sachsen* was not hit, and certainly not one of the Germans was hurt. Hansa Bay is a very small part of Greenland, but it was an enormous target from the air.

Dr. Weiss was in charge by the time the bombers came. He and Dr. Sensse and Schmidt and the other two men had got back from Ella Island after a journey of forty days. When they had found the house at Ella empty, they had stayed there for a week before they started their journey home again. They had come back by Musk Ox Fjord and had not thought of turning off to visit Mosquito Bay; so they were back at their base before they knew that Ritter had disappeared. They had been very surprised to find he had not come back; and Weiss had set to work at once to organise something which Ritter had never dreamed would happen: for Ritter, as a naval commander, had always planned to get the *Sachsen* out, and when it became quite obvious that that would be impossible, he had taken it for granted that escape was out of the question. But Weiss, who was not a sailor, appealed to the German Air Force to come to the rescue. When the American bombers came over, a German flying-boat was already waiting in the north of Norway, and some time in July, as soon as the sea-ice broke up and sufficient open leads of water could be seen, it came in and picked up all the men and took them back to Germany: all except one, whom they could not find. Before they left, they set Ritter's ship on fire. She melted a hole in the ice which still lay in the bay, and sank.

Later still in the summer, an American icebreaker forced its way up the coast towards Eskimoness, and at the same time Ziebell and Kurt Olsen and Marius, who had patched up the motor boat at Ella Island, were making their own way north. They came up Musk Ox Fjord, which was free of ice, and hauled a dinghy over the ten miles of land to the head of Loch Fyne, and rowed all the way down the loch and across to the desolate ruins. It was some satisfaction for the sledge patrol to cover the ground again without any help from outside, and to get back by themselves to the very place where their retreat had started; but the icebreaker got there first and it was the American crew who found the small outhouse full of furs, with the Danish flag among them and Ritter's defiant note pinned on the wall.

Afterwards the icebreaker went up to Sabine Island and steamed into Hansa Bay. Its crew had been told to look out for German survivors, but there was nobody there; nobody dead and nobody alive. The huts were in ruins, and the *Sachsen* was a stranded, burnt-out hulk.

36

BUT THAT was not quite the end of the whole affair. It ended in a rather mysterious way.

On the day after the icebreaker got to Hansa Bay, her captain gave shore leave to some of the crew and let them wander about the island. Some of them got as far as Germania Harbour, and while they were having a look at the old hunting station, a more primitive house than most of them had ever seen before, they were utterly astonished to hear music. Following the sound, they came upon an emaciated, bearded man, sitting on a rock, playing a phonograph. He was holding a hand-grenade, but made signs of surrender. The tattered anorak he was wearing had a bullet hole in the shoulder. He said his name was Sensse; but the name on his clothes, when they searched him, was Eli Knudsen.

Bit by bit, in his first few days in captivity on the ship, the Americans learned the outline of the story of this solitary enigmatic figure. It was in fact Dr. Sensse, who had been left behind when the Germans flew out of the country and was now discovered wearing a dead man's clothes.

When he and Weiss had got back to their base, it was nearly a month since they had left Ritter with Marius at Mosquito Bay. Everyone wondered what had happened to Ritter; probably some of them thought they were better off without him; but Dr. Sensse was not content to wonder. They had only just got back to the base in time, because the thaw had started and open leads were showing along the coast. But Sensse harnessed five dogs—not more, because they were short of dog food—and started alone for Mosquito Bay to look for the missing man; although Ritter himself, some months before, had given an order that nobody should risk his life for the sake of any one man.

It is not recorded whether Sensse ever got there. Somewhere on the way or on the way back, he met the disaster which anyone might have foreseen and which, indeed, he must have feared himself. The melting ice broke under his sledge, and he and the dogs and the sledge went through. He managed to drag himself out, but the sledge sank and took the dogs down with it.

No doubt in the warmth of the sun he had taken off his outer clothes and stowed them on the sledge; but he was not very far from Sandodden, and he succeeded in walking there. In the hut he found the clothes he had taken off Eli Knudsen to dress his wound when he was dying, and so he put them on.

He could not get away from Sandodden until the thaw was over, and during the weeks while he waited he lived there alone on the scraps of food which were left in the station, in the macabre company of the human corpse which he and the other Germans had left in the meat store. But there was an old boat at the station, and when at last the fjords were free of ice he launched it and rowed the fifty miles back to Germania Harbour, to find his compatriots gone and American sailors in possession of Sabine Island.

One is left with the question of why the German doctor risked his life alone on this dangerous journey. Did he go back out of charity, to bring help to Ritter, or out of patriotism, to arrest him? Or did he perhaps not want to escape to Germany?

One can make a few deductions from the facts. He only took half a team of dogs because of the shortage of food, and perhaps there was not enough food for another sledge; and yet it seems unlikely that he would have gone alone if he had been going as a Nazi, to corner Ritter and bring him back to answer for his crimes. Again, that was the winter of Stalingrad, when many intelligent Germans knew the war was lost; and Sensse, who was certainly intelligent, but was cut off from the spirit of resistance which still pervaded Germany, might have believed that Ritter had gone of his own free will and have chosen to follow him into captivity rather than fight on in a losing battle; and yet, in the end, he did make a tremendous effort to get back to Sabine Island.

The alternative remains that he went as a doctor and a friend, and risked his life because he imagined that Ritter was lying sick or injured or starving down at Mosquito Bay, deserted by Marius Jensen; and there is every reason to believe this is the truth. Perhaps as a doctor he had known all through the winter far more than Ritter had suspected of what was going on in Ritter's mind.

In the fight in north-east Greenland, diverse opinions of the morality of war had been revealed. Schmidt, whose dream of German greatness had been proof against the arctic charm; Ritter, whom arctic beauty had led back to the paths of God; Poulsen, Marius, Peter, Kurt and the others, who had loved the arctic peace and made war to preserve it as well as they were able; the Eskimos, whose whole world was pitched in the arctic splendour and whose whole morality was in the Sermon on the Mount: where among these did Dr. Sensse stand? The facts suggest that Sensse too, throughout that winter's night, had wanted to be offered Ritter's confidence and was ready in the end, though Ritter had held aloof, to acknowledge the noble tradition of the arctic by enduring the final test of human friendship.

So the story ended where it had begun, with a surprising encounter at the hut in Germania Harbour. On the day after it, the American ship steamed out of Hansa Bay, and Sabine Island was left deserted, as peaceful as it had always been since long before mankind began to fight. It is still deserted and perfectly peaceful now.

THE END

AUTHOR'S NOTE

One of the pleasures of writing a true story like this is that it leads an author to make a lot of new friends and acquaintances; and another pleasure is that it gives him an opportunity to thank them for their kindness.

I could not have begun to dig up the facts of what happened in north-east Greenland without the patient help of many people who were there during the war and told me all they could remember, especially the late Governor, Eske Brun; Ib Poulsen, Kurt Olsen, Marius Jensen and Carlos Ziebell of the Sledge Patrol; and Lieutenant Ritter.

I am also grateful to the Greenland Ministry of the Danish Government, of which Eske Brun is now the head, for permission to read official archives; to the Northern Mining Company for flying me to Greenland; and to many members of that company and of the Danish weather service and army for their arctic hospitality while I was there.

For photographs, it is my pleasure to thank Kurt Olsen, Colonel J. V. Helk of the Danish Geodetic Institute, Dr. Helger Larsen of the Danish Arctic Institute, Lieutenant Steen Malmquist, Christian Vibe, and Dr. Kaare Rodahl, the Norwegian explorer.

A great many other people, mostly Danes, have also helped me with expert knowledge of Greenland and of arctic affairs in general. Looking back on our conversations, I reckon that of each score of experts I have met, nineteen love Greenland and one, equally passionately, hates it. My own acquaintance with it has been shallower than theirs, but I have had time to begin to fall in love with it myself, and I hope the nineteen out of twenty will feel that their patience with me has been worth while and that I have managed to express the sentiment we share.

Perhaps readers of the story would like to know what has happened to the people in it since it ended. All of them, I am glad to say, are still alive and well, but all of them, except of course the Eskimos, have left the arctic now: on the whole, it is a very young man's country. Poulsen, who led the sledge patrol, and Ziebell, who was its senior man in Scoresby Sound, are both officers in the Danish Army, and live near Copenhagen. Kurt Olsen's home is also not far from theirs; but he is a navigator in the Scandinavian Airways System. The first time I wanted to see him, he was in Tokyo, the second time in South America, and the third time he was actually somewhere over Greenland on the way to San Francisco. This all added to the pleasure of meeting him in the end. Marius Jensen has his own farm now in Zealand. All these four are very much family men, with two or three children apiece, and have done their best to put their arctic love behind them.

Henry Rudi, the Norwegian, has retired from hunting now, and lives in the north of Norway. Peter Nielsen, who looked after Hochstetter Foreland for so long, has emigrated to Canada. It was he who was Ritter's principal jailer in Scoresby Sound, and I have heard a story which is so revealing of them both that I hope he will not mind if I repeat it. After the war, he heard that Ritter had fallen on difficult times, and he wrote to him and offered to lend him the money for him and his family to emigrate to Canada too.

But for family reasons, Ritter could not go, and he is still sailing as a merchant service officer. He still longs for the arctic. He would have liked to go back to Spitzbergen, where he had once been so happy, but the Norwegian authorities were understandably reluctant to let an ex-German officer go there; so he has never been able to see the arctic at all since he left it as a prisoner fourteen years ago. He and Poulsen have corresponded on and off since the war, and the writing of this book, I am happy to say was the cause of a friendly meeting at last between the two commanders. Ritter, like my other informants, told me the facts of what happened in Greenland as he could remember them, and left me largely to form my own opinions; and I think he would like me to add that he blames himself for what he did far more than I can bring myself to blame him. His ex-enemies, among whom I include myself, all wish him well; we all recognise the old truth which was shown again in that arctic spring of 1943: that it is proper for all true men of every nation to act together in opposition to evil and oppression, wherever and whenever they arise.

INDEX

A
American icebreaker
  crew discovers Sensse, 214
  traveling to Hansa Bay, 213
Angmagssalik colony, 6, 54
Aparte (Eskimo), 76, 159, 161
arctic living
  men's knowledge of, 27
  winters, 22–23

B
Balchen, Bernt, 211
Barselaisen, Josva, 159–61
bear hunting, 57–59
Bismarck (Battleship), 36
Brun, Eske
  agreeing with sledge patrol plan, 198
  assigning original sledge patrol,
    12–13
  background of, 8
  becoming ruler of Greenland, 9
  consulting Americans about protect-
    ing coastline, 10–11
  on Eskimos, 55
  first transmission from Poulsen to,
    79–80
  founding Greenland Army, 86–87
  giving new orders to retreat to
    Scoresby Sound, 157
  Jensen report transmitted to, 196
  ordering Ziebell to travel north, 156
  transmissions between Poulsen and,
    83, 85
  worrying about orders, 85
Byrd, Admiral, 211

C
Cape Wynn
  hunting hut, 68
  Marius Jensen remaining at, 73

Christian (Eskimo), 159
Clavering, Captain, 40, 54
crime, arctic, 20–21

D
daylight, lack of, 23
Dead Man's Bay, 54
Denmark, invasion of, 7
dog sledge
  commands, 25
  difficulties of driving, 25
  men's knowledge of, 27
  teams moved farther from Eskimo-
    ness house, 81–82
  trip preparation, 24
  weight limits, 26

E
Egede, Hans, 5–6
Ella expedition, 201–4
Ella Island
  Aparte and Mikael sent to, 93
  Ella expedition, 201–4
  interpretations of German
    sabotage, 204
  radio operator at, 76
  Nielsen and Jensen contemplate
    escaping to, 148
  sledge patrol, 12
  status upon expedition arrival, 203
Eric the Red, Greenland and, 3
Eskimoness
  bombing of, 211–12
  Danes feeling safe at, 92
  House described, 13
  description of, 13–14
  Eskimos feeling safe at, 92
  first winter, 23
  isolation of, 18, 29–30
  Jensen returning to, 78

responsibilities, 23–24
scientific station, 1–2
sledge patrol, 12
store ship arrival, 14
under attack, 99–100
Eskimos
  leaving Jensen at Cape Wynn, 73
  nature of, 55
  returning to Scoresby Sound, 158
ethics of war, 67
Evald (Eskimo)
  arriving at Ella Island, 127
  hunting, 77
  nervousness of, 95–96
  returning to station with Poulsen, 96
  sent home by Poulsen, 159
  tale of journey, 128–29
  traveling with Poulsen eastward,
    94–95

F
frostbite, avoiding, 108

G
Geographical Society Island, 40
Germania Harbour, 40, 69
Germans
  ambushing Jensen and Nielsen,
    140–41
  dog sledging knowledge, 88–89, 146
  fighting back, 212
  hunting with Jensen, 148
  leaving Mosquito Bay, 170
  leaving Sandodden, 144
  rescued/returned to Germany,
    212–13
  setting fire to *Sachsen,* 213
Godthaab's Gulf, 115
Greenland
  climate change, 4–5
  coastline protection, 10–11
  Eric the Red and, 3
  Eske Brun becoming ruler of, 9
  history of, 5

population of, 5
settlement established, 3–4
weather observation broadcasts,
  16–17
Greenland Army, 86–87

H
Hansa Bay
  bombers reaching, 212
  point of defence, 41
  Sachsen arriving at, 37
Hold With Hope
  naming of, 40
  patrolled by Kurt Olsen, 76
  Ritter and Jensen's travels, 166
hunting
  bear, 57–59
  huts for, 28–29

J
Jensen, Marius
  ambushed at Sandodden station,
    140–41
  arriving at Eskimoness after discov-
    ering Germans, 78
  awarded British Empire Medal and
    United States Legion of Merit, 196
  background of, 19
  chosen for Ella expedition, 199
  contemplating escape from Germans,
    147–48
  discovering Germans, 62
  encountering Eskimo hunter, 186–87
  encountering polar bear, 74
  encountering sledge patrol, 187–88
  explaining Swastika to Eskimos, 66
  finding note from Poulsen, 177
  finding Peter Nielsen, 135
  on his journey, 80–81
  hunting with Germans, 148
  journey to Sabine Island, 53
  journeys to Ella Island, 176–77
  journeys with Ritter, 163–67
  killing polar bear, 74–75

leaving for Kuppel Pass, 94
negotiations with Ritter, 152–53
ordered to Mosquito Bay, 167
ordered to Sabine Island, 51
promoted to sergeant, 196
questioned by Germans, 141–42
receiving old dog team back, 146
returning to Mosquito Bay, 191
spending night at Sandodden hunt-
    ing station, 56
starting back to Eskimoness, 135–36
staying behind at Cape Wynn, 73
tale of journey, 134–36, 189–96
told to look for Peter Nielsen, 93–94
traveling to Cape Wynn, 68
turning tables on Ritter, 171
waiting for Germans to leave Cape
    Wynn, 73
wrongly advising Germans, 170

K
Kaiser Franz Joseph Fjord, 40, 122
Knudsen, Eli
    death of, 139
    encountering Germans, 138
    finding Peter Nielsen, 135
    leaving for Kuppel Pass, 94
    radio operator at Ella Island, 76
    returning to Eskimoness, 81
    sent to look for Henry Rudi, 81
    starting back to Eskimoness, 135–36
    tale of journey, 134–36
    told to look for Peter Nielsen, 93–94
Knuth, Eigil, 16
Koch, Lauge, 15
Kuppel Pass, 135–36

L
Lars (Eskimo), 159
Loch Fyne, 40, 115, 166

M
maps (sledge patrol district)
    middle, 118

northern, 52
southern, 181
Maria Island, 40, 203
Mikael (Eskimo)
    arriving at Eskimoness, 80
    greeting Poulsen at Ella Island, 124
    journeys with Jensen, 53–54
    sent home by Poulsen, 159
Miss Boyd's Land, 40
Mosquito Bay, 167
Musk Ox Fjord, 122

N
Nazism, Ritter on, 35
Nielsen, Peter
    ambushed at Sandodden station, 141
    contemplating escape to Ella Island, 148
    encountering Rudi and Olsen, 133
    found by Knudsen and Jensen, 135
    guarding Ritter at Scoresby Sound, 205
    location during winter, 53
    questioned by Germans, 141–42
    returning to Ella Island, 160
    starting back to Eskimoness, 135–36
    traveling with Rudi and Olsen, 155
Nowotny, 45

O
Olsen, Kurt
    action station, 97
    background of, 19
    chosen for Ella expedition, 199
    encountering Peter Nielsen, 133
    log book found after war, 106
    patrolling Hold with Hope, 76
    returning to Ella Island, 160
    returning from Hold With Hope, 93
    signal transmission, 126
    tale of journey, 130–33
    transmitter going off air, 186

P
Poulsen, Ib
    action station, 97

alone at Eskimoness, 77
arguing with Ziebell, 158–59
arriving at Eskimoness station, 17
arriving at first hut after Loch Fyne, 121
arriving at Revet hut, 111–12
background of, 15–17
becoming leader of sledge patrol, 17
burying radio, 120
coming within sight of Ella Island, 123
continuing along fjord, 117–19
conversation with Ritter, 98–99
daily routine at Eskimoness, 77–78
difficulties after leaving Loch Fyne, 120–21
discovering missing brothers, 185–86
discussing defence plans with Ziebell, 183–85
doubts of, 84–85
events following attack on Eskimoness, 107–9
familiarity of route to Ella Island, 115
finding note from Henry Rudi at Revet hut, 112
first transmission to Eske Brun, 79–80
followed Ella expedition through radio reports, 201
giving orders to Eskimos if attacked, 96–97
greeted by Mikael at Ella Island, 124
interrogating Ritter, 198
journey to Ella Island, 115–23
journey to Scoresby Sound with Ziebell, 179
journey in Kaiser Franz Joseph Fjord, 122
journey in Musk Ox Fjord, 122
journey to Revet, 109–11
making station rounds, 97
meeting Ziebell, 157
ordering Marius Jensen to Sabine Island, 51
preparations to leave Revet, 113–14

raiding cache of supplies, 109
receiving machine-guns from American aircraft, 200
relationship with Ritter, 206
responsibilities, 18
returning with brothers to organise defence, 186
returning to Sandodden station, 96
route decision to Ella Island, 120
searching for Akre brothers, 178
sending Aparte and Mikael to Ella Island, 93
sending contingency to Scoresby Sound to take Nielsen's news, 161
sending initial radio signal from Ella Island, 125–26
sending/receiving transmissions with Eske Brun, 83, 85
sending Ziebell and Olsen to Carlsberg Fjord, 186
setting up depot on south side of island, 156
signaling Scoresby Sound from Ella Island, 126–27
signaling to expect American aircraft, 199–200
staying with Ziebell at Ella Island, 161
traveling to Ella to mend radio, 76
traveling with Evald, 94–95
trying to transmit to Scoresby Sound, 119–20
under attack, 99–100
waiting for answer from Eske Brun, 127
waiting for Ziebell, 156
warned about figure on ice, 97–98
weather expectations after Revet, 115–16
written orders buried, 82

R

Ritter
    arriving at Germania Harbour, 69, 147–48

background of, 33
becoming more sensitive to hostility, 46
as captain of *Sachsen,* 32
character differences with Schmidt, 42
collecting sledge patrol's personal possessions in hut, 105
contemplating outcome of journey, 173–75
contemplating reasons for hostility from colleagues, 47–49
conversation with Poulsen, 98–99
deciding to do God's will, 151
decision making processes, 90–91, 103–4
dividing sled dogs into teams, 145
encounter with Knudsen, 138
encountering sledge patrol as a prisoner, 187–88
entering house at Eskimoness, 103
excuse to winter in Greenland, 39
fearing for family safety, 46
first stop in Sandodden, 138
Gestapo affair, 33–34
interrogated by Poulsen, 198
journeys to Hansa Bay, 137
journeys with Jensen, 163–67
leaving message in Eskimoness hut, 105–6
left at Mosquito Bay by Jensen, 172
at Mosquito Bay with Schmidt and, 169–71
on Nazism, 35
negotiations with Jensen, 151–53
orders to establish meteorological party in Greenland, 34–35
orders Jensen to Mosquito Bay, 167
as prisoner, 197–98
questions Jensen and Nielsen, 141–42
reading Marius Jensen's log book, 89
recalling conversations with colleagues, 45
reflections during imprisonment, 207–8
refusing Jensen's request regarding Nielsen, 152
relationship with Poulsen, 206
removed to prison camp in America, 208
response to attack of Eskimoness, 101–2
returns old dog team to Jensen, 146
Schmidt and, 150–51
set Eskimoness on fire, 106
signaling headquarters about sledge drivers disappearing, 88
smashing radio at Eskimoness, 106
soldiers reporting to, 64–65
staying at Eskimoness, 104–5
struggling with Knudsen's death, 143
suspecting German cause, 44
suspicions of Schmidt, 44
treating Eskimo child for bullet wound, 208–9
warring with himself, 43
Rudi, Henry
action station, 97
as air-raid warden at Scoresby Sound, 205
at Clavering Island, 76
encountering Peter Nielsen, 133
found by Eli Knudsen, 81
hunting tale, 59–60
returning to Ella Island, 160
returning to Eskimoness with Eli Knudsen, 81
Ritter reads about in log book, 90
tale of his journey, 130–33
warning Poulsen of figure on ice, 97–98
Rudi's Bay, 40
rules of war, 86
Ruth's Island, 40

S
Sabine Island
bombing of, 211

description of, 39–40
named by, 40
Poulsen orders Marius Jensen to, 51
protection from, 38
trouble begins at, 41
Sachsen (trawler)
  crew of, 32
  during bombing, 212
  on fire, 213
  running aground, 37
  reached edge of ice, 35
  seeing aircraft, 38–39
  sending reports to German Navy, 41
Sandodden hunting station, 55–56
Schmidt, Dr.
  background of, 35
  character differences from Ritter, 42
  during bombing, 212
  following trail to Cape Wynn, 70–71
  greeting Ritter and Jensen at Mos-
    quito Bay, 167
  at Mosquito Bay with Ritter and,
    169–71
  Ritter and, 150–51
Scoresby, Captain, 40
Scoresby Sound
  acknowledging signal from Poulsen
    at Ella Island, 126
  American bomber over, 199–200
  defence system, 182–83
  description, 179–80
  discovered, 40
  settlement at, 54
Sensse, Dr.
  alerting Ritter to telegram, 46
  during bombing, 212
  tale of journey looking for Ritter,
    214–16
  treating Knudsen, 139
Shannon Island, 37
sledge dogs, cold and, 29
sledge patrol
  encountering Jensen and Ritter,
    187–88

at Eskimoness, 12
Eskimos at Scoresby Sound, 205
map of middle district, 118
map of northern district, 52
map of southern district, 181
members, 55
talks of advancing instead of retreating, 198
sledging
  best conditions for, 51–52
  Germans learning, 89
standards of morality, 20

T
tents, hunting huts versus, 28–29
traveller, equipment needed, 27–28

W
weather reports, German need for, 32
Weiss, Dr.
  during bombing, 212
  following trail to Cape Wynn, 70–71
  at Mosquito Bay, 168
  proposed plan to go to Ella Island, 153
  reconnaissance flight, 36
William (Eskimo)
  arriving at Eskimoness, 80
  journey with Jensen, 53–54
Wollaston Foreland, description of, 57

Z
Ziebell, Carlos
  arguing with Poulsen, 158–59
  arriving at Ella Island, 157
  chosen for Ella expedition, 199
  discussing defence plans with
    Poulsen, 183–85
  journeys from Ella Island to Scoresby
    Sound with Poulsen, 179
  meeting Poulsen, 157
  searching for Akre brothers, 178
  staying with Poulsen at Ella Island to
    cover retreat, 161
  transmitter going off air, 186